Bags Out At Seven

Bags Out At Seven

A Tale of Too Many Cities
(The Misadventures of a
Jaded Tour Leader)

ROBERT GLOBERMAN

Copyright © 2000 by Robert Globerman.

Library of Congress Number: 00-191159
ISBN #:   Softcover   0-7388-2376-7

All rights reserved. No part of this book may be reproduced or transmitted in any form or by any means, electronic or mechanical, including photocopying, recording, or by any information storage and retrieval system, without permission in writing from the copyright owner.

This book was printed in the United States of America.

To order additional copies of this book, contact:
Xlibris Corporation
1-888-7-XLIBRIS
www.Xlibris.com
Orders@Xlibris.com

Contents

1. FROM THE HALLS OF MONTEZUMA TO THE SHORES OF TRIPS 19
2. DEBT ON THE NILE 27
3. RSV— 39
4. THE PREFIX IN MISADVENTURES 43
5. CAPE MAY OR MAY NOT 71
6. A FEW BUMPS 79
7. AIRPORTS 85
8. ON MY OWN, OR, OFF THE BEATEN TREK 95
9. MY UNDERWEAR IS ALL OVER THE WORLD 105
10. TOILET TRAINING 113
11. STRAINED BEDFELLOWS 117
12. CLIENTELE/CLIENT HELL 127
13. SO WILL I EVER FIND SHANGRI-LA? 191
14. WHAT WILL I MISS? 205
15. WHAT WON'T I MISS? 213
16. AND NOW? 217

Dedication

This book is dedicated to my family, who, one way or another, labored through the trips with me. All my love to Regina, Bill, Whitney and John...

and to my grandsons, Bradley and Jason, whose coming into the world had something to do with my wanting to be at home now.

...and my sincere thanks to Robert Stewart, formerly of Prentice-Hall, for his suggestions and advice, his enthusiasm and confidence, his belief and encouragement, and his statement, "It shows ability, style and wit; it's significant and needs to be published," which was the carrot before my cart.

On another level, I would like to express my appreciation to all those who think they recognize themselves but are kind enough not to ask . . .

HOWEVER . . .

IF THE SHOE FITS,
GRIN AND WEAR IT.

"It was the best of times, it was the worst of times . . ."

As everyone knows, that's the first line of ***A Tale of Two Cities.*** My story is not at all related to the French Revolution, so far as I know. And I have no plan to do Mr. Charles Dickens an injustice by swiping his lead-in. In most ways, at most times, my life as a tour leader really was the best of times. What a way to spend one's retirement years! I was able to go all over the world, leading a group of people whom I, for the most part, enjoyed to the maximum.

But even the best of times can present problems. How often has one quoted Murphy's Law, that if something can go wrong, it will? Travel brochures tastefully display glorious pictures and glorious descriptions of glorious places. Few things are more irresistible than those shiny, full-color folders and brochures that entice us beyond resistance to fly off to those Edens that are scattered far away, where the weather is always perfect, planes leave and arrive on time, hotels and motorcoaches are pristine, tours and sites are superb, food is delectable, people are amiable, smiling, uncomplaining, gracious, understanding, patient, almost godlike . . .

Lest someone plans to run out and lead perfect groups all over the perfect world, this diatribe is meant to cast just a little light on the slightly darker side of tour leading. Diatribe is a strong word. I only mean–well, you'll know what I mean.

1

FROM THE HALLS OF MONTEZUMA TO THE SHORES OF TRIPS

My first foreign trip was to Mexico, about a hundred years ago. I hadn't been out of college very long, and I went with my mother as a kind of celebration of my graduation. Mexico was about as "foreign" as I was adventurous enough to go, knowing nothing at all about the ways of travel.

I went to the local travel agent and arranged a two-week trip which included merely the flights to and fro and hotel accommodations. Mexico City and Acapulco. That's it. No tours. Just that.

In those days, to get to Mexico, you flew National Airlines from Idlewild to Miami, then transferred to *Aerovias Guest* to Mexico City. My first flight. There was a short stopover in Washington, D.C., and National Airlines literally rolled out a red carpet for us as we walked down the steps from the DC-4-or-5 prop plane. Wow! First class.

When my mother and I switched planes in Miami (and I don't know how we did that without getting lost), we discovered there were only three other passengers: a young lady traveling alone, and two young men, students at the University of Mexico—all Americans. I did feel a little like I was on that plane to Shangri-La with Ronald Colman. I kept wondering why there weren't more fellow travelers this June—I never did answer that question.

Learning where we were going, the two guys said that when we got a cab at the airport in Mexico City and told the driver where we were going, whatever price he quoted, tell him it's too much. I made a mental note.

Upon arrival at the deserted, old airport late at night, we discovered the floors were flooded from a recent rain. Because we were the only arrivals, the procedure was simple and fast, but the scene was as dreary as a thirties movie of refugees fleeing Madrid or Shanghai. When the attendants applied stickers to our bags, they first bent down, touched the stickers to the wet floor and then stuck them on.

We finished formalities and went for the cab.

The driver put our bags into the trunk of the car as we got in out of the rain. He then took his seat as I said, "Hotel Reforma." Then I said, "How much?" He told me the price as he started the engine. I said that it was too much. He shut off the engine, got out of the car, opened the trunk and threw our bags out.

I looked around for the two helpful students. Neither they nor the young woman were in sight. Humbly, I said, "Okay, okay," and the driver once again placed our baggage in the trunk and we set off for our hotel.

Finding our way around the hub of Mexico City was no problem. I wanted to buy everything I saw, and I did manage to help the local economy. There was a pair of caricatured dolls I couldn't resist, and that started me, unknowingly, on my collection of a male and female doll in national garb, to represent each of the countries I would eventually visit; I couldn't resist a smashing pair of yellow(!) loafers made from horsehide; a silver watch (Mexico's so famous for silver) with a face of the omnipresent Aztec calendar, and with a silver band that turned my wrist green and black; plus the usual eye-catching merchandise designed for hayseeds like me: baskets, hand-carved wooden vases that said "Mexico." After all, wasn't it the sophisticated thing to do—buy the things that bore the name of the country? Oh, boy, Rube.

The streets of Mexico City were all broken up because major work on their sewers was being done following upon an epidemic of Hoof-And-Mouth disease. The name alone made me wonder if I should shorten our stay. I never saw a baby carriage. I did gasp at the number of old-looking, very young women with a missing leg, sitting on the streets, begging while nursing their young. Flies often hovered. The picture haunted me.

In our days in Mexico City we didn't do an awful lot besides walk around and buy whatever seemed unique and irresistible. Then we flew to Acapulco, which was the glamour-draw in the first place. Our hotel, the Caleta, was so new, it wasn't completely finished. It did seem like something out of the movies. (Everything seems like something out of the movies to me at sometime or other). The hotel was located on a high rise, overlooking the Technicolor sea, whose crashing waters we watched from our open-walled dining room. This was spectacular. Our room had its own terrace with a huge glass container of water for drinking. But it was always in direct sun. Who would want it? All the floors, inside and out, were ceramic tile, and servants scrubbed them daily. I think they were washed, tile by tile; or so it seemed. I wondered how there could still be those occasional small lizards scampering about.

Everything about the hotel was big and beautiful. The beach was another asset, though the sun-shelters were very far from the water, and you had to run to get into the water without burning your feet.

Well, you can't be as naive as I and be in Acapulco very long without an attack of Montezuma's Revenge. They were only words until it happened to me. Sounds "ignorable" in conversation. But when Montezuma does indeed decide to let you know that the water was not meant to be imbibed by you, his volcanic fury demands you return much more than you took, and violently.

My sin was great enough by itself, but it was compounded by the fact that the attack took place on a Sunday. That invited further wrath from the gods because nothing is open on Sunday, and nothing public runs to any place on Sunday, and the hotel staff does not provide for troubles on Sunday. The song, "Never on Sunday" really has nothing to do with Greece. It means if you're going to get sick in Mexico, nev . . .

Simple and almost laughable as an attack is to talk about after the fact, having been unable to leave the bathroom long enough to say I have to return, I understood the ability of Montezuma to conquer Mexico. The agony I experienced was enough, way back then, to make sure never to be casual about the precautions necessary in many places I have subsequently visited. Ever since then, whenever I hold orientations for groups who travel with me, I etch on their minds the possible horrors that could befall them if they are careless in their dietary habits. At least, when I got hit, my time and schedule were my own, and flexible.

I never did learn why the hotel did not keep on hand whatever medication I did take, whether it worked or not. My recovery may have been just the old savior, Time. Today, of course, a number of miracle remedies exist. Back in those dark ages, my concern was whether my mother, who seemed to have been by-passed by Senor Montezuma, would be able to make the arrangements to get my body back home for burial or would she just find a local cemetery.

All through the trip and long after, it seemed to me that I had gotten everything from that virgin "foreign" trip one could imagine, laying Sorry Sunday aside. Long, long after, reading, listening, learning, I realized I must have missed a good deal, not having had any kind of itinerary or "itinerizer". But I've already called myself a hayseed. After all, weren't organized trips just for ladies with blue hair? Also, why should anyone expect to do something like a foreign trip correctly the first time? Well, the uncertain halls of Montezuma lay behind me; ahead were the "sures" of "Trip"-oli. But I didn't know it then.

The typical trip I lead averages twenty-five people. Of the twenty-five, twenty are women. Of the twenty, fifteen are happily married women whose husbands just don't travel, so two happily married women travel together. The remainder of the group are single, widowed, divorced and separated women, also doubling up, with just a couple of single roomers. The age range is mostly from the forties to the seventies. Almost every passenger is bright, educated and interested. They don't look primarily for beaches and scenery; rather, they want museums, cathedrals, historical landmarks and the unique. The average person takes one or two trips with me each year. Out of the twenty-five, twenty are repeaters. Mostly, they are wonderful and down-to-earth. They are accepting of each others' foibles and tolerant for the two weeks, or whatever the length of the trip might be.

Almost never has a man been on a trip without having been with his wife.

I can recall only once when a man came alone, and only once have two men traveled together.

A newcomer can be spotted immediately when she (and I must say "she" because that's how it is) says something like, "When I was on my fifth trip to Paris, or was it my fourth? No, I think the sixth" . . .

The regulars, I'm happy to say, never try to impress. The biggest dud on a trip is the one who finds the need to enumerate travels, unaware that the good guys find no such need, in spite of equal experience.

There are also the "impression-makers" who say this is their first group experience. He or she is used to renting a car and doing it on their own, not liking to be tied to a group or a schedule. Now, I understand and appreciate that, but that's not what they're telling me. They are telling me they're too sophisticated to follow along with a group and have someone else "itinerize". I repeat that traveling solo or as a couple is a logical way to travel, and, for some, the only way. But those in my experience who've traveled that way have subconsciously told me how much they missed, and how much time they spent in making arrangements. I'm happy to say that after they've done our "group thing", they've acknowledged the joy of relaxing in knowing that all details and connections have been worked out for them, and they don't miss the time lost in parking or missing roads, having tours pre-arranged, instead, with guides waiting at the sites and all. To have to conform to a time schedule is a small trade-off for all the conveniences included.

Having traveled so much because it's "what I do," I can say I've traveled independently and with groups, and I prefer, mostly, groups. I have not done my own driving because I just plain don't want to. There's enough driving at home. I want to be able to look at everything, not road signs and maps. I don't want to have to concentrate on how to get there; I prefer seeing more.

Because I work out my own itineraries, the groundwork is laid out months and months in advance. I have to know when certain galleries are open, when the crowds are smallest, when the weather is best, when special hotels have accommodations, which roads are preferable, when to be centrally located and when to be away from the hustle-and- bustle.

One woman who has taken a number of trips with me said at the conclusion of our first Italian trip together, "I just realized how coordinated everything is: the bus takes us to the sites, and it's there, waiting for us when we're done. There's no looking for transportation. Meals are ready to be served when we get to the hotels and restaurants; no waiting or having to make our own reservations. I've just taken it all for granted."

Well, at this point I've got to acknowledge that the reader might think I'm trying to promote my trips. Forget it. I don't promote. Or I like to think I don't. I'm merely in favor of group travel. I don't know how other professional tours satisfy their customers, but basically group travel is designed to offer the maximum, and if you find a good travel organization, it's worth sticking with. In my own case, because the thrust is museums, cathedrals and historical sites, those who like my style feel confident enough to keep returning. Their faith keeps me conscientious. How can I let someone down who's come to expect a particular level of excellence? I'm too insecure to be able to accept losing a client.

Besides, I've retired now, so why would I promote?

I would like it known that I've had the most marvelous times, leading these trips, and, for the most part, it has been an enviable career. I can't possibly recall the number of times people have said, seemingly joking but obviously serious, "Can you use an assistant?" The question has been asked in a variety of ways by a surprising selection of people; what they mean is that they'd like to travel free, as I have done, and they think it's an exciting, even glamorous life, both concepts correct, but not quite as they imagine. Number one, with the excitement comes an enormous amount of groundwork. Putting together a trip is not a simple matter, and one would be hard put to realize the labor to get it together, to get it going and to handle the incredible details necessary to do it right. The glamour? If being acknowledged as the person responsible for herding a couple of dozen people through crowded bazaars and souks and plazas and airports and on and off buses is glamorous, well, then, they shouldn't use that word to describe Lana Turner, as well.

The homework never ends. One way or another, I've been a student all my life. I'm a natural "studier". I get latched on to something and find I pursue it like a detective on the trail of the mystery of the age. Relentlessly, I must find the answer for questions no one has yet asked. As an art historian/lecturer I have always felt that I must anticipate every conceivable question, so I prepare myself ruthlessly. People ask about technical details that I delight in explaining. But, in order to do that, I drive myself mercilessly, hounding libraries and finding clues that lead me on pursuits I didn't dream of when I began. It is certainly no way to relax, and the major deficit for me is that I have acquired the miserable inability to relax. I do not know what the word "relax" means, and I am definitely not happy to admit this. But I have learned to accept my nature. As my wonderful wife Regina tells everyone, if she and I decide I must take a nap on the living room couch, two minutes after I lie down, my gaze travels to the ceiling, where I notice a crack that needs repair, and off I go. Transplant that to anything else I do to try to relax, and projects seem to present themselves and call me. It's pathetic.

Well, to get on with it: I pick a place I want to visit in depth. Having been involved in art history all my life, I don't have to start at square one to create a trip. But there is an itinerary to conceive. The trip must be plotted in such a way as to cover the maximum with a minimum of traveling, except in cases where the actual traveling is as much a part of the discovery as seeing the sights. I choose all the exciting churches, museums and landmarks I can, and then I determine what kind of scheduling can include them all. When are the best times to visit the places I want to see? What is the logical routing? How best to get from A to B and B to C? What is there on the way that should be included that I might not have thought of? How much time do I think we need at each sight? How much time can people have for photographing? for buying? How can there be enough, but not too much, time at a place? How do I please the wives who buy and their husbands who don't? Where will we eat? What about the pit stops (excuse me, the "technical stops")? Are we at a place accessible to the buses? Well, that's part one of a hundred-part test I take.

I'll get on with the first trip. Starting with the next chapter, the technicalities will come up from time to time in my description of various trips and people. *Avante!*

2

DEBT ON THE NILE

I had been teaching art history as an adjunct assistant professor in Marymount College in Tarrytown, New York. Marymount ran special degree programs for adults, The Weekend College. I cannot praise it highly enough. The course offerings were exciting and unbelievably varied. The classes were terrific: very motivated, bright people who had full-time jobs but were taking these college programs to get a degree and to advance in their jobs. They never had to be encouraged to study for tests or to get their homework in on time. Their industry was an inspiration to a teacher. Term papers were beautifully executed. Test results were, by and large, excellent. Class participation was what teachers always hope for. I was stimulated by the discussions that happened in every session. In the teacher evaluation that came at the end of every term, the students praised my enthusiasm; yes, I'm enthusiastic by nature anyway, but much of the enthusiasm on my part came from the enthusiasm of the students themselves. I was excited to meet these classses, to present information to groups who hungered for it.

It was inevitable, I suppose, that the students in large numbers requested that classes be held on-site. The Weekend College had, in addition to its regular classes, workshops which sometimes took place off-campus. In my own case, I'd been leading weekend trips to such places as the Wilmington, Delaware area, in order to visit Winterthur, Nemours and Hagley Mills, all of which tied in with a course I was giving in American architecture, and each of which is a memorable museum of the finest American architecture and artifacts, showing the development of that area by the DuPont family.

All the slides and textbooks available cannot offer what one gets from being at the actual site and seeing the subject "in the flesh". With the wealth of knowledge these vital students brought back to the classroom, term papers were a joy to read. I suggested alternatives in approach. They could, for example, report on their findings in the style of a detective novel in which a fictional story could be illustrated through the facts they were required to present. They could write a journal in the style of a diary of someone living at the time, such as a servant in the mansion, taking note of the furniture the care of which was their responsibility. I didn't want typical dry regurgitation of facts they'd picked up. Creative writing with the required information distinctly presented was more motivational for them and much more exciting for me. And their papers were knockouts. I asked them ahead of time to have more than one copy: (1) I hated to make my corrections on something that was visually beautiful and more than just a report, and (2) I so often wanted to keep a copy (and I still have them). It's impossible to measure their excitement as they set about the task. A teacher's delight. They went beyond the necessary requirements of the paper, often illustrating with beautiful photos they'd purchased for the purpose. They were turned on and so was I.

So—I guess it was kind of significant that I planned a trip to Egypt and they planned to take it. It honestly was that innocent. I had been toying with the idea of leading a trip to Egypt for some time. It had come about as follows:

For some time I had been doing slide-lectures on art history and foreign countries. I was doing them for libraries, museums, woman's clubs, church groups and the like. It was customary at the end of each program to have a question-answer period. One night, while doing a program on Egypt in one of the town halls, someone asked an oft-asked question, "Do you ever lead trips to the places you talk about?" As usual, I answered, "No, I don't." From the rear of the auditorium, a small, elderly man yelled out, "I've been following you all around the county, listening to your programs. Somebody always asks you if you lead trips, and you always say 'No'. When the hell you gonna say 'Yes'?"

He intimidated me. Small as he was, I didn't know how to handle the directness, so I just spontaneously said, "Okay. Yes. Where do you want to go?"

He said, "Well, you're talking about Egypt! Take 'em to Egypt!"

Not knowing what else to do, I said, "If anyone's interested, just put your name and address on a piece of paper and give it to me on your way out." I hadn't the slightest idea what I would do after collecting them.

Several people handed in the information I had requested. The little man was not one of them. Nor did I ever see him again. He was, somehow, a benefactor—at least he was my catalyst. And I never even had the opportunity to thank him. And that's actually how it all began.

I'd retired from the Ossining School system and was teaching at Marymount only to keep my finger in. Just the Weekend College every third weekend, and I wasn't interested in doing any more than that. I'd been a high school teacher for twenty-seven years before that, and I'd officially retired. Marymount was to keep the adrenalin up, that's all. (I couldn't know it would be so fulfilling). Anyway, since I had time and had always wanted to return to Egypt with Regina, I decided that leading a group would be a way for me to be able to go without financial cost.

Having decided to take the step, I mentioned it in class. The students responded positively to the idea and asked if they could get college credit for such a trip, just as they did for the weekend trips. I told them I'd ask the Dean. When she learned the requirements would be just as legitimate as for any weekend workshop or any class, she gave wholehearted permission. A weekend trip was coming up; on the bus on the way, I made the announcement. There was a roar of acceptance, and everyone wanted the details immediately.

Not knowing, in the first place, what kind of response I would get for the trip when it got down to the essentials (everybody can say they're going, but registering is a different story), I reserved thirty spaces with the airlines and hotels. In less than six weeks—six months ahead of time—the trip was sold out. Several Marymounters signed up as well as people with no connection to the college who'd heard about it. This was in the summer, and the trip was planned for the following February.

I decided to have an orientation for the trip, a month before departure. Marymount graciously consented to the use of their library, and the group showed up enthusiastically en masse. And now, to Egypt:

Upon arrival, we were met in the airport by our foreign company representative, a son-of-a-bitch named, oddly, George (an Egyptian named George?).

As soon as we met, he told me that someone from a previous group had left a suitcase, and there was no way to get it out of the airport. Would I accept it as one of our group members' in order to get it out? I answered that of course I couldn't do something like that. He insisted that it was perfectly all right. I mentioned that if it was all right, there had to be another way for someone to do it, and that he had to know I couldn't and wouldn't claim it as one of ours.

We departed from the airport without the questionable luggage and met our tour manager and guide. That was all of George for the moment, but we would meet again, regretfully, to justify my cursing.

Our tour manager was a darkly handsome, young Egyptian man named Ahmed, who stood six feet five inches tall. Inasmuch as I had almost all women on this trip, I was delighted at his appearance, because his height would make him visible in crowded places and his looks would keep the women from getting lost. So much for quick judgments.

Ahmed's main responsibility was to get us from city to city, hotel to hotel, site to site, making all transfer connections smooth and comfortable. Arrival and departure times were his obligation.

As handsome as Ahmed was, our guide, Sahar, was beautiful. By any standards one would have to enjoy this woman who had movie star loveliness. How could this be? Two movie stars? She was a knockout. Egypt certainly knows how to grow them. What a pair, and what a non-match.

It was Sahar who gave the running, in-depth commentary on every historical site we visited. Well-schooled, as is required by the Government, she fascinated the group who drank in every word she uttered.

It could have been merely a vacation for me. There was no teaching necessary because of the completeness of Sahar's enriching narration. Only when there were points necessary for classroom context did I add to her documentary. Graciously, after her talks at each site, she would smile and ask, "Professor Bob, would you like to say something here?" And when I did, she would always say kindly, "Oh, that's interesting. I must add that when I lead my next group."

We proceeded on our way, checking into our lavish hotel and setting out for the typical three-day tour of Cairo and its environs, including Saqqara and Giza, the whole pyramid scene. This was to be a ten-day all-inclusive trip, covering everything except Alexandria. It's possible; it does work; it's not a case of "If this is Tuesday, it must be Belgium." And I emphatically told everyone not to drink the water or eat salad or uncooked vegetables or fresh fruit, and to take a spoonful of Pepto-Bismol first thing each morning. Memories . . .

In Egypt you very quickly learn that the popular catch-phrase is "No problem." Were that it were so!

On day 2, Ahmed said he wasn't feeling well. (By the way, the spelling of his name is with an "h", no "c", but it's pronounced "ACH-med"). Well, we had to stop at an occasional pharmacy for Ahmed to find something suitable for his cold-or-whatever. The following night we were to attend the "Sound-and-Light" program at the pyramids in Giza. Our bus driver, a kindly, elderly, proper man, was in the hotel lobby at the designated time, but there was no Ahmed. The driver spoke no English at all. Between the two of us, we managed to scout out the entire area in search of Ahmed. (Beautiful Sahar was not a part of this evening's activities, so we didn't have the back-up of her presence). I had no way of reaching Ahmed. No one at the desk could help. Finally there was no time left for solving the mystery; the driver volunteered to take us without Ahmed, obviously nervous about doing this on his own.

We arrived at the site, our bus one of ten million, at least. All the tourists we hadn't seen anywhere converged on Giza for this show. Somehow we got our reserved tickets and got in to see the impressive show. It was truly thrilling to stare at the Pyramids and the Sphinx and listen to cavernous sounds of music and narration and watch different colored lights as they played upon the monuments. We had been advised that it could be cool in the evening despite the oppressive heat of the day. No one took that advice terribly seriously, but we were grateful for whatever extra clothing, such as our winter jackets from the U.S., because those desert nights do get starkly cold. I remembered well from years before.

My concentration was less than perfect because I kept wondering how we would find our driver once we left. His looks were nondescript; I wasn't sure whether he understood where we were to meet; all those endless people; could I be sure not to lose anyone? Could he possibly have taken off? Was I over my head? Sheez . . .

I need not have worried. In spite of the throngs, our faithful driver found us. The glee on his face was a joy to behold. The whole group was together, and we got on the bus. Since the driver had no right to take us without the tour manager, he was visibly nervous. I could sense his relief in finding us, and, in his own timid way, he offered to take us to some sights we would not normally see, such as Sadat's tomb. When we arrived there, in pitch darkness, he approached the militia at the heavily guarded site, told our tale and got permission for us to visit. The man was humbly shaky, yet excited about this bold gesture he'd made.

The group was very touched by his efforts on our behalf and took up a collection. Had it not been for his untried bravura, we might not have had monument coverage. This was Cairo, not Manhattan. Severe protocol exists here. Our driver overstepped the boundaries of caste. What kind of trouble might he have made for himself?

When I presented him with the group's show of appreciation, he removed his hat and thanked us profusely—and humbly. We said we'd see him in the morning, hoped he understood and went inside. Within five minutes, he reappeared. Apparently he had taken the time to see how much money we'd actually given him and felt this called for a much greater expression of appreciation. When he found me, there was perspiration all over his face, he was crushing his hat in his hands, and he cried as he voiced his gratitude. My god, we couldn't have given him that much, but I'm sure we remain in his memory today.

Everything about a visit to Cairo and the Pyramid complex at nearby Giza is as thrilling to visit as anyone could hope it would be. The Cairo Museum houses a collection that impresses even those most blase. The mosques are captivating. Sahar's commentaries were as wonderful as she was beautiful. If she merely listed the entries in a telephone directory, she would have been entrancing, but it happens that her lectures were superb. There is no way not to feel you've seen it all when you visit the Step Pyramid at Saqqara and, of course, the three Pyramids at Giza. It's as if it's too unimaginable to exist, and then there you are, telling yourself you cannot believe it. I never lost the thrill of my first visit, years earlier. Now I re-lived it. I'd been teaching Egyptian art, culture and history for countless years; what a treat to know that visiting now was so gratifying for those students for whom all that study was really coming to life.

It is natural to want the things that thrill you to thrill others. There was no question here and all through Egypt. I would guess that Egypt remains the favorite of most of the people who have traveled with me through the years. The majesty of such unique structures, the thought that they were created so long ago, the exotic mystery attached to all of them, the stories of the pharaohs, the coming to life of all those things you'd read of, dreamed of, seen only in movies—it's quite stirring.

Entering Chefren's pyramid, the middle one of the three, was certainly some piece de resistance. I deliberately had not assured the group that they'd be able to do that. It isn't necessarily open at all times; it isn't something you can promise. But they did get to go inside, and I know they'll never get over it. Some of the papers they wrote took us back inside, because their intrigue inspired the fiction in them to create stories that led them back there. Having lunch in view of the pyramids, at the famous Mena House, was also a fine tidbit.

After three days, it was time to fly to Luxor, where we were to board our boat, which would be home for most of the remainder of the trip. Ahmed, whose job it was to handle reservations, seating, luggage and all the non-educational portions of the trip, maintained a pathetic, sorrowful look as he accompanied us, brow in continual furrow. He apologized enough times and mentioned that he thought he might have an abscessed tooth. His skin shone from perspiration. He always looked clean, but there was the constant appearance of sweat.

We managed to have no difficulty in getting seated on the plane, but its departure was delayed by hours, causing our arrival in Luxor to be after dark, not the original plan at all. After collecting all our luggage, Ahmed got us on the bus which took us to the banks of the Nile, where our boat awaited us. The spot where we left the bus did not seem convenient for embarkation. Sahar told Ahmed that we had to get to a stairway located elsewhere. Ahmed insisted we were in the right place. They had a discreet argument; Sahar conceded unhappily. Thirty people were waiting for them to come to some sort of settlement. Technically speaking, Ahmed's rank was superior to Sahar's. That was error number 625.

When it was pointed out, we were able to see our *Golden Boat*. The moon provided our only light. The question was: how do we get from the high bank down to the boat, when it was difficult to know what lay three feet ahead? Ahmed located what might be called a path. A steep one! It appeared to be neither clear nor very traversable. With extreme care, we all began to descend. I got to the boat as soon as I could, in order to be able to lend support for the others. At the bottom of the embankment, a couple of sailors waited to lend a hand to enable the passengers to walk across a narrow plank from the land to the gangplank of the boat, a peculiar, awkward, dangerous transfer, crazy, insane, thoughtless. The two sailors stood on the far end of the ramshackle plank and grabbed the hands of each passenger as the passenger, laden with his own carry-ons, was handed over by two men in our group on the near side. The plank in question was no more than a foot wide, about eight feet long and far from new. Between the land and the gangplank was the water, the Nile. Our first real view of the Nile was this eight-foot gap of water into which we prayed not to fall.

One of my passengers was a heavy-set woman who wore two hearing aids. I suddenly thought of the effect of sound on balance. I feared that she would lose her footing. The sailors on the near side held her firmly as the sailors on the far side took her hands. At that precise moment the plank cracked loudly. The men zipped her quickly onto the gangplank as the board plunged to the water below. Gasps and yelps echoed. Allah be praised, she was safe!

A replacement board arrived; everyone quietly and stealthily got transferred from land to boat; luggage arrived as well, and finally we were all safely ensconced in our new surroundings. I estimated my weight loss to be about equal to my hair loss.

In the bright light of the following morning, we noticed, from the still-docked boat, that the concrete stairs Sahar had tried to locate were within thirty feet of our treacherous path. We had unnecessarily gone down that irregular, littered, rugged path a stone's throw from stairs that were there just for the purpose of boarding the boat safely. Ah, Ahmed, Ahmed.

Afterwards, everyone treated the mishap like a great adventure, and their stories were probably retold more often than descriptions of our sites. And the woman under whom the plank had cracked was a perfect sport throughout the rest of the trip.

Ahmed continued to suffer, to the point where one wondered whether he needed more sympathy than he was getting. This formerly handsome giant spent most of the visible sailing time slumped in a chair with blankets pulled up to his chin, while the rest of us wondered how little we could wear in order to be cool enough to withstand the February heat. At one point he asked if he could wear my sweatshirt. I had bought it in Cairo, and it said, "No Problem."

Each time I sat down to eat, Ahmed would appear at the entrance to the dining room, catch my eye and crook his finger at me, beckoning. He always seemed to need to talk to me about some trivial detail when I was in the dining room. The group wanted me to enjoy myself and seemed to want to protect me from Ahmed's intrusions. Sahar tried very hard to be diplomatic about Ahmed even though, day by day, she was handling more and more of his responsibilities.

I prayed that whatever Ahmed's physical problem was, it was not contagious. I didn't want anyone to get sick. Should I burn my new sweatshirt? Was his increasing lethargy related to his doses of medicine? Will he last through the trip? Sahar's tact and taste prevented her from disclosing too much information beyond the history of Egypt.

We visited the Valley of the Kings, with everyone duly impressed by Tut's tomb, unimpressive as it is, compared to others'. The temples at Karnak and Luxor were as thrilling as they ought to be. And then we flew to Abu Simbel. A short flight and a two-hour visit. Thrill of a lifetime. I truly don't understand tourists who go to Egypt and don't include Abu Simbel in their itinerary. It's not an expensive option, and when you're already in the neighborhood . . .

I had lectured in class and on the trip about the historic relocation of the temple complex at Abu Simbel. The mechanics involved were enough to stun anyone. The subject had been moved from an area two hundred feet forward and lower down. The history-making disassembling of this monumental structure had been the subject of at least three issues of *National Geographic* alone, in the 1960's, lushly illustrated with photographs from every conceivable angle, showing in detail how it had been cut apart and moved to a higher location, piece by numbered piece. Even without its historical and aesthetic architectural value, the entire reclamation process was thrilling from an engineering point of view. Here we were, at the already moved site. Regina and our kids and I had been here exactly ten years earlier. Here was a second chance to see the fabulous area. The thrill does not dim.

Well, after nine days we had covered all we'd wanted to, and I repeat my claim that one can really see Egypt in ten days. If you want to belabor the point, of course it would be good to have more time. There's almost no such thing as spending as much time as you want, if you're someplace you love. Can a vacation be long enough, regardless of where you are? It was time to return home.

Ahmed and Sahar had said goodbye and were not to accompany us to the airport. Only the driver was with us. I never saw Ahmed again. I did learn that he married and became a father the following year. In exactly a year I repeated the trip, and Sahar was not only our guide but our tour manager, as well, something she had doubled up on toward the end of this first trip. She and I corresponded for a couple of years, during which time she referred to me as her brother. In the last letter I had received from her, she wrote that her family had found a husband for her whom she hoped she would like. She asked me to pray for her. The correspondence did not continue. I hoped she married a man she loved, and I did pray. I know no more about her. She was special.

The group and I had flown back to Cairo for our final overnight, and, after an early rise, we were back in Cairo Airport, surely the most crowded place in all the world. Going through customs and immigration was a bit of a hassle, with everyone's luggage having increased in number and bulge, having bought a large portion of the country in various forms of arts and crafts and tourist treasures.

At some point in the long waiting, I told as many of my group as I could find to go ahead and check in; I would handle their luggage with the porters. Well, unknown to me, my friend from point of arrival–sly George–had managed to dismiss the porters and place himself on the other side of the entry way, where boarding passengers and luggage had to go. George was smiling a sinister smile. I was not mistaken; it was not a smile-smile. I asked him to assist me with the bags and entry; that was his purpose, that's what he had been paid to do. He informed me he could not come to my side of the entry. I told him he had been able to do so when we arrived. He told me that was then, this was now. I told him I had two dozen bags with me, my group had gone ahead. His answer was, "You know how to get rid of the crowd, don't you? Just yell BOMB!"

I asked how he could say that to me, and the slit-eyed, one-sided smile he gave sufficed as the answer. This was my punishment for not having accepted that dubious bag upon arrival.

Jack, the terrific son of the terrific woman under whose weight the plank had cracked while boarding the boat at Aswan, called to me from over the crowd. He and his wife had noticed the contretemps with George, surmised correctly that something was amiss, got a couple of the men from our group who had not yet boarded the plane, and quickly enforced an over-the-head system of passing the bags through. In a matter of minutes (sweaty minutes, but wonderful minutes), those many suitcases that surrounded me zoomed to the conveyor belt that would send them onto the plane. Finally, Regina and I got into that delicious line being checked onto the flight.

The last person I passed before showing my boarding pass was George, who gave me the pleasure of one more look at his evil smile and said, "It could have been easy."

My response will go unrecorded here.

The handful of my group who participated in this rescue operation gave me a sweaty smile of approval as I entered the plane, and a hundred years from now I will vividly see their faces, bless them as I have done countless times, and smile my own special smile of love.

I see Jack and his wife once in a while, and though nothing is said about the incident, I automatically see the scene in the airport, wondering if I'd still be there if not for them, and I silently bless them all over again.

3

RSV—

The idea for the orientations I hold for my tours came from nowhere. I did not know of anyone doing them; they aren't copied from another source. I merely thought, the first time I did a trip, that doing so might be a good idea.

I decided to hold each one on a Sunday, a month before each trip, at two in the afternoon. This was so that there would be daylight in which the people could find my house, since I live in a suburban area. And with their lasting three hours, there would still be daylight when they left.

I would direct traffic as each car arrived, in order to get everyone sardined in a driveway not meant for so many cars. The average trip had thirty people. Even with coupled travelers, there were usually about fifteen cars at the least.

Regina would always prepare refreshments, trying, as much as possible, to have things that were native to the country or countries we would visit. The first half hour was spent with introductions, since all did not arrive at the stroke of two. Then for forty-five minutes to an hour, I spoke, explaining as much as possible to prepare the people for what they would encounter in the country to be visited: customs, currency exchange, weather, health precautions, how not to get lost, what to do if one did, purchasing and anything peculiar to that country. I suggested how to pack, what to take, what to leave at home. I repeated the old saying, "Lay out all your clothes and all your money; leave half the clothes, take twice the money."

I show my suitcase and explain why I have that type. I tell what I pack. I tell them to take twice the medication they require, placing one half in their luggage, the other half to be carried on their person, in case of the loss of either half. "If you wear glasses, take an extra pair in case–. Carry a photocopy of your ticket and passport identification page in a spot other than where you carry the original, which means the copies go in the luggage. Bring a hat with a visor, a rain poncho, etc."

We discuss the importance of promptness because, obviously, everyone must be on time each morning and for each tour. Motorcoach etiquette is discussed: not taking possession of a particular seat each day; rotating seats but not by regimen; not speaking while the guide is speaking. And if the guide is not speaking and you *are*, learn to stop in the middle of a sentence (you can always get back to wherever you were) when the guide does begin. Of course there is no smoking on the bus; I request that the smokers get out of the habit of standing at and smoking near the door when they *are* outside (smokers are often unaware of or unconcerned about the smoke going into the bus).

The use of the toilet on the bus is always mentioned. People are told that, of course, the toilet is for their use, but if they can wait till the next pit stop, it's preferable in order to avoid odors. Emergencies, though, are emergencies, and everyone complies.

Someone always asks if I will recommend reading matter, and I do, from travel guides (I do have my favorites) to anything related to the country. And there are always people who eagerly recommend books *they've* enjoyed. The average traveler does a lot of preparation, I'm happy to say.

The list goes on and on. Much of what I say is obvious; much should be; someone always expresses appreciation for the pointers.

There is a stock statement I make without fail: "There are three things you cannot lose. In descending order of importance they are your passport, your return ticket and *me!* The reasons should be obvious."

Questions follow, and often some of the veteran travelers add to the list. It's all very helpful, and newcomers appreciate the special tips.

Following the question-and-answer period, I show a video of the places to be visited. Sometimes I get them from the government tourist offices, sometimes I buy them; I do make sure they are quality films that don't merely commercialize, but, rather, show what we will experience, in the best form available. The video takes close to an hour.

At the end of the video, the people stretch and mingle and indulge in more of Regina's delicacies. By this time, three hours have passed, new acquaintances have been made, and people feel much more prepared for the trips.

When I send out the announcements for these orientations, I send them with a letter asking that I be notified as soon as possible whether or not they will be coming. After all, there is a good deal of preparation involved. Thirty people in the house requires some furniture rearrangement; Regina prepares a substantial amount of refreshments; I alert my neighbor about the overflow of cars—-. An illustrated map is on the reverse side of the letter, with the day, date and time clearly listed. All I ask is that I be informed as soon as possible about attendance.

So you can guess, now, what I'm up to, right? There is always someone who does not tell me anything. Occasionally that is the person, too, who comes with an unannounced (and uninvited) guest who is not going on the trip. Sometimes it's a woman's husband, and I understand he is driving her to this affair, but that's two people I still need to know about. It's nice enough of Regina and me to accept someone who isn't on the trip; at least let us know. I can't tell you how often that happens—in spite of the clarity of the message.

Adding fuel to this fire: In the beginning, and for a number of trips in the first couple of years of leading trips, we also held a reunion *DINNER* a month after our return. It is okay to wonder, at this point, if Regina and I were out of our minds. Regina prepared a complete dinner in the style of the cuisine of the country we'd just visited. She was, at the time, a full-time teacher who, out of the goodness of her heart and the absurdity of my mind, did this because it seemed like a nice idea at the time.

Again, there were those—not necessarily the same—people who did not respond to the invitation. I assumed that no response meant no attendance. (I've more than proven my stupidity by now, have I not?). Not only did they attend, but, again, guests were brought. Where I didn't expect even one person to come as a result of no response, I got two. Everyone ate with great relish. Many—including the unknown and uninvited—left with no thanks or comments.

Every camel's back waits for a particular straw. There was one trip on which Regina did not accompany me, but, being the incredible sport she is, she prepared dinner for the masses anyway. I'm focusing right now on one couple who came, partook, and never even said a word to Regina, as if she were the cook or the maid. Up until this time, these wrongs annoyed me a great deal, then aggravated me. Now I spit nails. I asked Regina where that particular couple was, and she said, "I think they left."

"Did they not say they were going?" I asked.

"Not to me. I thought they must have said something to *you*."

They had left, and left their plates for us servants. That was the last reunion dinner we ever had. A couple of times someone would ask why we weren't having them any more. My reply was, "Would you like to do it?" Occasionally, but only occasionally, someone would invite the group, but, of course, there was nothing that would approach a dinner–or a lunch–or an impressive arrangment of anything. There would be coffee and finger things. Well, that's fine, really, but I will say I've kissed Regina a number of times, with the question, "How did I ever let you do that?"

I've mentioned this to some of those who have been close to us. They always said they didn't know how we did it all in the first place. When I mentioned the callousness of those who never responded and/or brought guests to boot, their answers ranged from "That's *chutzpah*" to "That's balls."

Funny, I guess reunion dinners started in response to a passenger on the first trip saying, "We should have a photo-reunion, where we all get to see and exchange pictures", and I was stupid enough to be the one to pick up on it.

4

THE PREFIX IN MISADVENTURES

I could spend my life describing the glories and beauties of foreign lands. I've been to almost every country in Europe, and many times to most. I've been to a good deal of the Far East, several times to China alone, including Hong Kong. I've seen a large share of the Middle East and Northern Africa, and a trip to Peru gets me to include South America. And I've been Down Under. When you do this much traveling, and when you're "in the business", to boot, certainly you read everything there is, before long. Having done that, I would never have the courage to attempt to re-invent the perfected wheel. In what new way could I describe the Taj Mahal or the Pyramids or the Great Wall? How many movie remakes live up to the original?

If this is a travel book of some kind, it would seem reasonable to expect some regular descriptions or stories of the many places to which I've led trips. However, I am irregular, this book is irregular, and the anecdotes that follow will have to be in the same category.

I would like to state emphatically that as groups go, I think no groups are better than those from the U.S.A. As every barrel might contain a rotten apple or two, so may every group contain a stinker or two. But as a group, I think we are by far the most congenial and considerate. If three groups of different nationalities are on a cruise, and dinner is buffet style, and groups are to line up, the Americans are the most generous in not pushing or elbowing. Experience has shown the French to be at the opposite end of the judgment scale. Sorry. Ask around and observe for yourself.

The Japanese are the most visible and the most smilingly congenial. I understand merchants catering to them all over. What buyers! I will always remember being with my group in the Delft factory in Holland. Most of them were in the "seconds" room of incidental items, wavering over already reduced prices. The entire Japanese group was in the area with the largest, most lavish ware, buying in large quantities and without question.

Most groups stay by themselves, and that's to be understoood. However, I see so many Americans making sincere efforts to engage others in conversation. And they are gently, smilingly courteous. I think that's overlooked in view of the occasional over-outspoken attention-grabber who gives us all a bad name. We really are, en masse, jolly good fellows.

India

I had not done many countries by the time I led a group to India. I'm fortunate that my following has been a loyal and trusting one. I explained that India was a place I very much wanted to visit, but I hadn't been there. I'm known as one who does his homework, but would that be enough? I wouldn't be able to tell the group anything from first-hand experience. Is that okay? As I think back on it, I have no idea where I got the nerve. Imagine leading a group halfway around the world on an extremely long flight to a country you had not visited. Well, I did just that.

I have a rough time with cigarette smoke. Our takeoff from JFK on Air India was delayed because the plane was late in arriving, due to fog in Delhi. Waiting in the airport was difficult for me because there was such excessive smoking, and it was difficult to escape. My group was small, less than twenty, but many were new to me, and I felt it was important to be available for them, so I could not disappear.

When finally we were seated on the plane, I found myself in the middle section, next to an Indian couple with an infant. They spoke no English, oddly. After we were underway, the child filled his diaper. The odor could have been a war weapon. The parents did nothing about it. After some time, I built up the courage to ask them to change the diaper.

Communication did not happen. I asked the airline attendant to convey my message. She told me it was not her responsibility. I explained that I would accept the responsibility if she would merely explain for me. She half-heartedly told them something.

I looked at the couple, pointed to the baby and pinched my nose. They smiled.

When nothing more happened, I put my hands together as in prayer, tilted my head and said "Please" in every language I could muster. They only shrugged.

We were to land in Heathrow Airport in London. I thought, perhaps, the hour layover would somehow find a solution. Upon arrival, we were informed that, due to unusual crowdedness in Heathrow, passengers flying through to Delhi were to remain on the plane during the one-hour layover. Ohmygod. I'd say "Shit", as usual, but I didn't want a reminder.

Delhi was years away. I don't drink alcohol, so I was unable to escape that way, and there were no vacant seats. To be away from my seat, I talked to as many of my group as I could, something I do not normally do, as I don't like to stand in the aisle.

Arrival at Delhi was supposed to mean we could enter the airport, which really meant we could leave the plane before continuing to Bombay. However, to try to make up for some of the time lost due to the fog, there was no time there, either. Onward to Bombay.

I had been doing my share of coughing from the overexposure to smoke back in JFK, but somehow I guess I got through that. I prepared for getting the group through the airport in Bombay. I almost did not care about whatever involvements that would mean, for what it *really* meant was that I would be on land for the first time in almost a day, and away from smells.

I got the group through Immigration and Customs without incident. I do remember, though, that as of that trip, I advised anyone traveling with me to wait in any line except the one I'm in. Whichever line I pick, it seems, has the inspector who goes to lunch, walks away or dies on the spot.

I always, always have the fear that our guide or liaison will not be there to find us. I have yet to take a trip without that worry. Our guide, as always, was there. We would begin touring immediately.

I never want to waste time, but I was a zombie at that point and feeling sick from the smoke, the diaper load, the aggravation and the longest flight I had ever taken. But I refused to let anyone know.

To this day, parts of our trip to Elephanta Island are as hazy to me as the everpresent smoke. This was January. How welcome the heat was going to be after a New York winter. On the steps of the pier, waiting for the boat, among many sweaty bodies, I thought I would collapse from the humidity. On the boat from the Bombay Harbor to the island, my coughing condition expanded to include a running nose and sneezing. These things *never* happen to me. Why now? What will this group think? I'm the leader, for God's sake!

Our hotel was a five-star beauty which is almost totally blank in my memory. I can only recall falling into my bed and passing into sleep, knowing that it was an ungodly hour at which we would be leaving in the morning for a city tour. This was the one poorly planned part of the itinerary because of which I would advise anyone taking a trip to India to have the first day at leisure. This, from a guy who wants no free time.

I sleepwalked through the first full day in India, in Bombay. Happily, that's the only time that ever happened to me, but I wish it hadn't. The group was wonderful about it, and, fortunately, by the next day I was totally recovered.

From Bombay we flew to Udaipur. As one who never wants to be idle and does not need to sit and relax, I have to say this is one place where, if I were confined to a hotel, I could manage to enjoy it to the utmost. Our motorcoach dropped us at the edge of the lake at which we embarked on a small, old-fashioned, canopied boat that chugged us out to the Lake Palace Hotel, which won my heart before we even entered. The boat drifted right up to the steps which rose from the water. The hotel was its own little island, beautifully tiled, with no two rooms alike, where it was a joy just to go and visit everyone's room. Wow! People lived like that? Ah, to be a maharajah. Any guide book will give you the gorgeous picture. What a place. A palace on the lake, literally *on* the lake.

Touring was what touring is. Our guide took us to all the places listed in the brochures, and our time in Udaipur was perfect.

When we arrived at the airport for our flight to Jaipur, we were asked by India Air, not Air India, if anyone had batteries of any kind. Most people's cameras had batteries, of course. We were told no one could have batteries with them on the plane, for fear of making bombs. I mentioned that we were not told this on our flight from Bombay to Udaipur. "You should have been," was the reply.

Our luggage was already on the airfield. I, as the leader, was required to collect everyone's batteries and take them, under guard, to the airfield and place them in my luggage. Having collected dozens of batteries of different makes and sizes and types, there was no time or way to put each person's own in his own luggage; I had to place them all in mine. There was no way I could assure the group that each person would get back his own. That did not matter heavily; as long as they would get back what *seemed* to be the right one.

I returned to the group, dripping with perspiration, and we waited a couple of hours for our one-hour flight.

Upon arrival in Jaipur, we were bussed to our new hotel, another masterpiece of Taj architecture called the Rambagh Palace. Totally different from the Lake Palace, this new temporary home was almost ranch-like, but in the grandest manner. We entered the hotel via a grand exterior stairway. Once inside, we had to get to our rooms by going down a flight. It sounds simple enough, but the corridors were dimly lit and mysteriously lonely.

Upon entering my accommodation, I was stunned at its vastness. A foyer led to a bedroom on my right, beyond which was a sitting room the size of an average living room. The bathroom was a step up and large enough for three pool tables. When I entered the dimly-lit sitting room, I discovered that the windows, which ran the length of the room, were only slightly above ground level, overlooking a lawn that ran on into woods. Outside, the lighting was dim, as it was in the corridors. The whole arrangement felt spooky, and I admit to being uncomfortable.

I tried to bolt the windows, because all kinds of eerie, murderous thoughts crowded my mind. I was unable to. I called the desk and asked for someone to come to do it. When the chamberman came, he asked me why. I was embarrassed to tell him, but I did. He managed to bolt all but one, saying he could not get that one to work.

My bedroom was a room away from the sitting room, with half a wall permanently open. After I got into bed, I had to acclimatize myself to unique sounds and try to act like a big boy, not the Nervous Nellie I truthfully felt like. Here I was, in a spectacular hotel, worried about an unlockable window, shadows and sounds. Eventually I did fall asleep.

We were met early the next morning by our guide who reminded me of Sal Mineo. Short, dark, swarthy and animated, he immediately said to me, "When we take the people into the emporiums, we get thirty percent of what they buy. You take fifteen and I take fifteen."

"I'm not comfortable with that," I replied. "I know these people. They're not strangers, they're friends. Can't *they* get the discount?" I naively asked.

"No. The only way they could get it is if you give one percent each to fifteen people, instead of taking your own."

Of course I should have known this from being in the business, but, oddly, this was the first time a guide had been so direct. Occasionally in the past, I would get a break on a purchase because of being the leader, but when faced with a monetary payment based on the purchases of the group, I had difficulty, so I just refused.

I did get a better price on occasional items I bought throughout the trip, but I was unable to accept a percentage that came from the group's purchases. If they had been strangers to me, I probably would have turned around and agreed to it, but I have to live with myself, and I was unable to "take a profit" from their buying.

Wherever we were taken, and there were several emporia throughout the trip, it was obvious that the merchandise was of the highest quality, and I soon learned that here is where there is not enough time for some of the travelers and too much for others. It is not a totally workable situation for that very reason. One learns to watch the salesmen in their various, though similar, ways, try to entice the prospective buyers, whether through a dramatic posturing with irresistible carpets or through having a woman from the group selected as a model while demonstrating the draping of a sari. All merchandise was appealing; all showcases were stylish; all merchants were smooth.

Every item seemed to have someone in the crowd to whom it spoke, and people do buy. One can look at a huge carpet and say, "I'd never be able to get it home," and in a minute, two men move with speed and grace to show how easily it gets folded into a small package and *Voila–isn't that even more tempting!*

I guess it was in Jaipur that I became convinced that the odor was distinctly potent and permanent. It was the result of burning dung. As we drove through countryside and villages, we were aware of Indians carrying stacks of wedges of dried dung, selling it as fuel. Dryness of throats is a common occurrence in the confined air of a bus in a place like India or Egypt or China. The smoke and pollution are difficult to escape. Non-smokers like myself are particularly susceptible to the ill-effects. It's important to carry water and hard candies. And once someone in the group picks up a cold, I am reminded, as I remind my people, that nothing travels faster than a cold on a bus.

Chloe, a woman about sixty, became enamored of our guide. Chloe had a certain grace and femininity that reminded me of Vivien Leigh in *THE ROMAN SPRING OF MRS. STONE*. She'd mentioned that she'd lost her husband, the love of her life, a year before, and there would never be another like him. She was a well-educated, articulate, graceful woman, the type who would be asked by a merchant to model a sari, and she would eat up all the false praise.

Somehow this almost glamorous, but foolish, woman became attracted to our Sal Mineo and informed her roommate, whom she did not know before this trip, that she would not be flying with us to our next stop, Agra. Instead, she was remaining with Sal and coming with him a few days later by bus, in time to see all the sites and be with us for the rest of the trip. He was our guide only in Jaipur.

Astonished and concerned that she had not let me know, I had to inform her that I was responsible for everyone on the trip; how could she expect to leave in the middle and catch up with us? How could she feel safe in doing this? Did she really think this through?

She sincerely and kindly offered to write a letter, relieving me of any responsibility or obligation. A friend of hers on the trip assured me that I was not the only one thinking she was unraveling, but she was, after all, an adult, and I had no way of preventing her from doing what she was doing. So she stayed– with the understanding that if she never caught up with us, I could not become Stanley to her Livingstone. The group gave me their assurance that there was nothing I could do and I was not to feel responsible, and on we went.

All the while I worried. Would she be safe? Would she get some deadly disease? Would she return to civilization? Is she out of her mind? Am I out of mine? She's with a guy young enough to be her son, screwing around in *INDIA*, this woman for whom there had been only one man.

We did head on for Agra, the place most people want to see because it is the place of the Taj Mahal.

I have always been able to enjoy ruins more than pristine beauty, but with all the pictures and all the preparation, the Taj Mahal certainly impressed me as the most absolutely beautiful building I had ever seen. The approach is dramatic in itself. You know what you are about to see; the motorcoach drops you off at the rim of the site; you walk to a large stone building which serves as its entrance. Once through the building you have the perspective you have always seen: the impeccable structure beyond the reflecting pool. You stand there, using up an entire roll of film and then proceed to pass the pool and climb the stairs of this magnificent wonder. It is necessary to remove your shoes, and that is certainly reasonable. Then you have the thrill of walking in and around the most incredible structure you can think of. Inside, down the stairs to view the tombs is very humid and stuffy, but to stroll around the mosque itself is a thrill of dreams that recurs for me regularly. All that great white marble.

Our stay in Agra was long enough for Chloe to arrive. We did not get to see Sal Mineo again, but Chloe seemed to exhibit a recharged battery, so I was happy to think all went well, that it was somehow worth it, and, mostly, that she was safe.

I celebrated my birthday on this trip, the only time I was ever in two different countries on the same day for the occasion. We flew to Varanasi where, early the next morning, we bussed to the outskirts of the city before dawn. We were dropped off more than a mile from our destination, the Ganges. There was no way for a motorcoach to get through the crowds heading where we were heading. Bikes and three-wheeled tuk-tuks were the only vehicles that moved. Throngs of people walked as we did, though only we looked like us. The Indians were on their way for the early morning ritual, involving bathing in the polluted waters of the Ganges.

When at last the river was well in view, we were on the top of an extremely wide flight of numerous stairs leading down to the water. It was a scene from a movie, of course. At the bottom, our guide had arranged for a strong, sizeable rowboat-of-sorts for us. We entered and spent the next two hours drifting along the shore, never more than a hundred feet from the thousands of people in various forms of bathing outfits, from bikinis to bedsheets. The sun slowly rose, illuminating the scene in various tones and tints. The odor of burning dung was not disturbing, and the ritual bathing seemed quite natural. I was lost in the mysticism of it all, while trying to capture it on film. I expected to be looked at as an invader, but the ceremony continued, oblivious to us. That morning comes back to me more than most.

When those who followed my travel career learned I was going to India, the common comment was, "Oh, I don't want to see the poverty." No other country aroused that comment, but I heard it over and over. I have been more aware of poverty when trying to step over sleeping bodies outside Port Authority in New York City. In India it is called poverty; in New York it is called the homeless. At least the people in India who slept out-of-doors were not struggling against the cold.

Learning about Buddhism and visiting Buddist temples among others, I recalled my all-time favorite movie, **Lost Horizon**. I had read the book, as well, of course, but it is the movie which has stayed with me. I had first seen the movie when it was re-issued at a time when I was twelve. It is the only thing I can think of which was a favorite and has remained so. The original effect never wore off. The only thing different when I watch it these days, which I do, from time to time, is that, of course, I know what's coming. But I still feel the excitement I felt when I saw it way back then, the thrill never having been equalled.

As I wandered through this country of India, the mesmerism took hold. And then we flew to Nepal for the second half of my birthday, celebrated that night at our hotel.

The next morning we ascended the mountains from the top of which we gazed toward Tibet, where **Lost Horizon** took place. My longing eyes took in the Himalayas, and I was reminded that that was the place I have most wanted to visit, that I knew I would never see. While on the mountain tops, looking over lushly terraced greenery, I turned into myself and understood why James Hilton wrote of Shangri-La as being in this area. All my history and experiences had been mundane; though Egypt, a special dream of a place I once thought I'd never see, was all that I had hoped, this place mysticised me. Those things happen to other people often and in places I have visited, but it is not something that happens to me. There are several places where, in my experience, I gazed in awe. Several. But in Nepal, and more recently on Machu Picchu in Peru, the magic that others feel regularly and easily at last reached me.

Our Nepalese guide took us to a home on the side of the mountain in which a couple lived with the husband's mother and the many children he and his wife had. On the ground floor was one large dirt-floored room which served as all the public rooms of the house. A ladder led to the second floor, with living space exactly the same size, divided into two rooms, one for the couple, the other for everyone else. No bathrooms, no kitchen, no closets. There was one electric light, one bulb suspended from the low downstairs ceiling. There were almost no furnishings, primarily mats to sleep on and a large vase-like, woven container of grain. Alongside the house, a stream ran down the mountain, next to the road. That water served all water needs. A small plot of land was in front of the house, and on the side was a garden that supplied almost all their food. The whole house was immaculate, and the cooking was done outside.

The entire family was barefooted and happy to have our company. They were happy, period. They had next to nothing that would be called material goods. But they were so happy. There was a strong temptation to give them everything we carried, but there was also a matter of their dignity. We did give the children candies and pens, even paper. I wanted so to give them money in order to purchase what I, foolish I, thought they might want. But they so obviously had everything they could want. East is east, and west is—well, east is east.

Nepal was very eastern, different from India, cleaner, more mysterious, crowded with temples everywhere. After a few days, we flew back to Delhi, our last stop before the long flight home.

When we flew from home to India, I knew that I wanted to buy a large brass tray to serve as a table top. I had asked the flight captain where I might put it on the return flight. He told me to be sure to have it wrapped well, and it could be placed behind the last seats before the bulkhead. That was reasonable and agreeable to me. He told me to tell that to the customs people on my way out of the airport coming back.

In Delhi we were taken to an impressive emporium whose director told me many celebrities bought there, and he mentioned, in particular, Elizabeth Taylor. In a matter of minutes, I saw the irresistible tray of trays. It was four feet in diameter, with the center section sunken, like an oversized rim plate. It was solid brass, on which a million flowers were worked in enamel, looking like cloisonne. I was informed that two men worked on it daily for two months. It was more beautiful and elaborate than I had expected, a piece de resistance. This time I asked if my leadership could get me a good reduction in price. It cost eight hundred fifty dollars at that time, and I could have it for three hundred fifty. Back then it seemed like a lot of money, but I had to have it.

I explained the need to have it wrapped well. They told me not to worry. It would come to my hotel the next day, prepared for its journey. And the next day, it indeed arrived, well padded and wrapped in Delhi cloth (burlap). Because of its shape and size, it could not stand. It could not be placed flat, either. It was carried to my room, and when we left Delhi, it had to be carried out when we headed for the airport.

One of the women in the group, Eileen, has been one of the most special people of all the groups. She was extremely well-traveled and observant about everything experienced. She was one of those rare people who need no attention but who are appreciative of everything that happens. She wastes no words, speaking only when she has something to say, and what she says is something worth hearing. She has a totally good sense of humor and goes with the flow, making the best of every situation. She had bought a papier mache Christmas tree ball. It was about eight inches in diameter and weighed nothing. It was unique in its decidedly Indian design, and I enjoyed the pleasure she derived from having found this object.

When we arrived at customs in the Delhi airport, I explained to the inspector that the plane captain had said I could take the tray on board to be placed at the bulkhead. The inspector told me it would have to go with the luggage. I said I was afraid to have it with the luggage since it could not stand, and if it were placed flat and luggage was put on top of it, it would be ruined. He said it would go with the luggage. I repeated my message from the captain, and the inspector repeated his decision. One more volley was all we could manage. I was given no choice, and my precious tray was somehow carried to its place with the luggage.

Meanwhile, Eileen was stopped with her Christmas ball and told it had to be X-rayed and she would have to remain in a separate part of the waiting room. She told them then to keep the ball, rather than be separated from everyone. They insisted that, no, it would be X-rayed, and she must stay near the X-ray machines. I refused to leave her alone, so I got word to the others, and I remained with Eileen.

Close to an hour later, the call was made for passengers to begin boarding. The X-ray screens showed what they had been showing for an hour. I went to the most official-looking person I could find, explained that I was leading this group. Everyone had boarded, I could not leave Eileen, and I would not board without her. His expression never changed.

A dignified Indian lady was being detained for film she had purchased. Strongly, she told them to keep the damn film, she wanted to get on the plane. They ignored her, as well. She shouted, "I bought the damn film myself; I have the right to leave it, if I please! I'm from this country; I know what I can do and not do!"

So I got salty too and said to the same official, "I'm here, leading a group. I'm a travel agent. I will be speaking to an organization of all travel agencies throughout the United States as soon as I get back. This woman with me has been trying to get on the plane for the past half hour. Get us on now, or I'll be telling every agency in the States to stop all travel to India! Do you understand?"

Sooo–- I lied a little.

As nothing was said to the Indian lady, nothing was said to me. I got Eileen and said, "Come on. We're getting on that plane NOW. Let someone try to stop us. This is ridiculous. If we keep waiting, there won't be any overhead space for our carry-ons. The Indian woman just walked through."

We got on the plane. We should have acted sooner. We did not wait for Eileen's ball. The plane was packed. Eileen's small carry-on never made it into the overhead storage compartment, but it served her later as a place to rest her head when she decided to cradle her head in her arms, leaning forward, halfway through the endless flight.

It is my custom to wait in the home airport (usually, as in this case, JFK) until everyone with me has collected his luggage and made his way out. Somehow, Eileen's Christmas ball, that thin papier mache feather of an object, appeared in the crowded airport on a ledge. It had traveled with us and managed to arrive in perfect condition. She was happily surprised. ???

Now everyone was gone. I had my luggage, but no tray. I walked to the wall where the conveyor belt enters the building and looked through the straps, outside. I watched luggage being tossed from carriers to the ground, shuddering. But there was no tray. I did feel there was no way for it to enter on the conveyor belt because it could not stand on end and its width was too great to lie on the belt. It was the width of the raised sides of the system. No way could it enter on that belt.

Finally I spotted a giant of a man in a turban, Punjab come to life. Was this a sign? He looked very imposing and official. I approached him and told him about the tray. He said to wait. He vanished in the direction of the tarmac, and in five minutes he reappeared with my four-foot tall package.

I tried to tip him, but he refused. He got more thanks, though, than he had ever heard. Now I went with difficulty, with the cumbersome, heavy tray, my luggage, my expanded carry-on and whatever would not fit in those pieces, and headed for customs. When I finally made it to the inspection officer, clunking every minute, looking like an Ellis Island refugee from another generation, the inspector pointed to the four-foot burlap-wrapped monster and asked, "What's that?"

I explained.

He said, "Well, get it out of here. You're holding everyone up!"

The words were blessed; I did not care if he did bark. I was on my way out of those swinging doors that would lead me to the waiting, smiling faces of my family.

There they were, relieved to see me, not worried, because the others who had gone ahead explained why I was delayed.

We exited into the below-freezing January of Kennedy Airport's parking lot and realized when we got to the car that this fabulous tray, which had presented so much trouble, could not fit into the car. I had thought it would stand on the floor of the back seat, but it would not fit through the door. We removed the bags which had just been placed in the trunk and tried to get it in there. It fit only one-third of the way. Well, there was nothing we could do. We could not tie it on the roof. There was no rope (which I've learned now never to be without), and even if we could have tied it on, the fierce wind would have made us airborne.

One way or the other, we managed to secure it in the trunk, though more than half protruded. We drove home at half-speed to prevent leaving the ground. The twenty hours of grueling flight were becoming a memory, because home would be sweet home.

The table whose legs are heavy camel's legs and whose glorious enameled top is this heavy brass tray is the conversation piece of the room it occupies, a room filled with equally unusual objects of art, most of which have stories as crazy as this one.

China

The first group I ever took to China was the first group of strangers I ever led. And I had never been to China. A large travel company that specialized in the Far East offered me the opportunity to host a group there, and I looked forward to it with great anticipation, negative and positive. Negative because I didn't know the ropes there and didn't have the security of the group being people who trusted me no matter what; positive because the creation and the pre-arrangements were all done. I did not have to come up with itineraries, mailings, phone calls, orientations, and, if they didn't like something about the tour, I wouldn't feel personally responsible.

I was given a six-page sheet of instructions, advice, pointers and other data. I was also given a list of passengers with their visa numbers, birth dates and addresses. One passenger, Gail, was a travel agent, and next to her name was a note telling me to give her the red-carpet treatment. First name on the list was my own, followed by *VIP*. Second was Gail, also followed by *VIP*. There were several copies of the list, one for each of the hotels. The list was numbered, and my notes told me to have the people, upon assembly at the Immigration desk in the Shanghai airport, in the order in which their names appeared, so they each had a number.

It had been a very long flight. I flew from New York to San Francisco, where I stayed overnight. The next morning I met the passengers in the airport in San Francisco. We then flew to Taipei (about thirteen hours, as I remember) and then on to Shanghai, another three hours.

I lined everyone up according to the listing and took it upon myself to ask a uniformed officer in the very crowded Immigration section if I could have my group in a line of their own, since they numbered thirty, suggesting that it might be easier for the inspectors, when I really thought it would be easier for us. I waited to flinch in case I raised his anger at my nerve. Instead he signaled us to our own line, and the process was smooth. I had to retain a particular copy of the passenger list, stamped and initialed in red, in order to be able to leave the country at the proper time.

Gail, whose voice was rough and New Yorkese, of course was always next to me because of the numbered system. She was very talkative, with laced language and many opinions, which were usually negative and always strong.

The Shanghai Hilton was a typically deluxe 5-star hotel. I made a point of memorizing everyone's names. Fortunately, having been a teacher for so long, I was good at names. At breakfast I greeted everyone by name, and I sensed their appreciation. I had to be honest enough to tell them this was my maiden voyage to China; it upset no one. However, Gail saw to it that we were seated together for breakfast, and at dinner that night, when I left my room to head for the dining room, she was in the corridor, waiting for me. Our rooms were adjacent, due to that numbering system, and I always give out my number anyhow, in case someone needs me.

Our stay in Shanghai was pleasantly uneventful, my strongest impression being our visit to the Palace School for gifted children, which we visited on a Sunday, when the place was packed with eager, talented children painting, sewing, singing and playing musical instruments in winter jackets to withstand the cold in the unheated building. Watching tiny ballerinas perform without having to be told to smile, listening to a chorus sing "Edelweiss" without being certain they even understood the words, listening to a child too small to be able to reach an octave, playing Mozart without an error, all brought tears to my eyes. They were brilliant. These children spent a non-school day doing extra work in school. Not only were they gifted and talented, they were sweet and beautiful. In the courtyard, many handed us their names and addresses on a piece of paper and asked that we write.

All the sites were memorable and exciting, but years later, when I think of Shanghai, and I have been there a few times now, I think of the poignant two hours spent in that most special palace with those most special children.

Following one of a few traditional tourist package routes, we flew to Beijing. Our wait for rooms at the Kempinski Hotel was brutal. Nothing was ready, and they did not have enough rooms anyway, having overbooked. When I insisted that they move faster because the group was getting angry, they said there was another plane arriving, and they had to have rooms for them as well. I had to get forceful and ask what the sense was in making a group that was already there wait for another group to add to the confusion. And six women had single accommodations which they discovered to be a room with a convertible sofa for a bed. They protested en masse, and I backed them up. After two hours and much anger, the room situation did work out, but it would not have, had things been left as they were. I was worried that the travel company that sent me on this trip would object to my getting forceful with a hotel they regularly used, but I rationalized that they would prefer their clients be happy.

When I was old enough to travel, one way or another I set my sights on three obvious landmarks that were beyond my dreams: the Pyramids, most of all; the Taj Mahal, only because it was like a dream castle; and the Great Wall of China. I honestly never expected the dreams to come true.

Just about every tour group that goes to the Wall goes to the same point. A long, pleasant bus ride takes you to one common point of entry. It has become the mecca for all those who visit the Wall. Since one walks it at his own pace, this was my first chance to be somewhat on my own. At Tiananmen Square and the Ming Tombs we had stayed together; that was not possible at the Wall. Some climbed, some did not; some went in one direction on the Wall, some in the opposite. Our guide told us what time to meet at a particular point, and we were on our own.

I climbed the Wall in great excitement, silently saying over and over, "I'm here, I'm here." As always, the memories built up from a child's lifetime in the movies, history rolling across my mind's eye. I was especially happy to be alone here, of all places. I climbed to the highest point visible from the starting point, and the point where most people stopped. The Wall, after all, goes on forever; you stop where you want. I started in a cotton turtle neck, topped by a sweater, topped by my ski jacket. It was March. Halfway up I removed the jacket, and at the top I removed the sweater. I don't remember that the weather had warmed up. Rather the energy and excitement did it.

Upon returning to the active areas where we were to board our bus, and having more than half an hour to the good, I took advantage of the competitive prices and did a fair share of shopping. Since, like a typical tourist, I buy a sweatshirt (where possible) that represents the country, I found the incredible buy of huge, soft sweatshirts that showed the wall with the caption "I Climbed the Great Wall" for three dollars apiece!

Now that we had been in China a few days, I was used to the fact that almost no one in the group liked the food. Wherever we ate, in or out of the hotels, the food was always served on a large lazy Susan with what seemed to me to be a large variety. But they all complained. I found enough to please me. It all seemed inferior to the Chinese food we know and love in the States, but I found no problem. Except: I love soup, and all the soups were lukewarm and tasteless.

Gail came with a case of canned tuna and a can opener. In almost every dining situation, she pulled out a can of tuna and did not even try what was on the table. She also tried to sit next to me at all times, and she was not enjoyable, merely loud, raucous and foul-mouthed, unaware of the negative impression she was leaving on everyone, each of whom said something like, "And she's a travel agent?"

There were evenings of special entertainment in buildings that served as restaurants and theaters. Food was lavishly arranged on dramatically decorated tables, and here one could have all the varieties of food imaginable. Also, here there seemed to be no complaints. There were also times when, for no reason I could fathom except the cost, the bus took us from our own hotel to the dining room of another hotel, where the food was no different from the food no one liked elsewhere. Because of traffic it often took an hour to get there and more than that to get back. The buses in China were far from elegant and new, and complaints began about that. Complaints also began about the number of Friendship Shops and Emporia that we were taken to. Even the perennial shoppers complained. The commercialization accounted for that. The guides' kickbacks from shoppers encouraged them to make these stops, but the saturation point entered and planted a kink. In truth, the number of the commercial stops did get intolerable.

Everyone goes to Xi'an since the underground terra cotta army of Emperor Qin Shi Huang was discovered in 1974. The life-sized figures and horses, numbering about 7000, are certainly mind-boggling and worth the visit. The display leaves everyone in awe. Certainly the Forbidden City in Beijing is awesome, as well, but there there is the vast area through which everyone's enthusiasm gets dispersed. In the roofed vault that contains the terra cotta army, there is something of a hushed appreciation.

Nearby are small shops and stalls where wonderful folk art is sold in the form of intriguing tempera and watercolor paintings, so entrancing that I had to buy enough to fill more than one wall of my house. Paintings of ducks and geese and landscapes and children in snow suits were to grace my home.

The traditional tourist overview of China generally includes a cruise on the Li Liang River, a four-hour delight along the unique shores which, in the Guilin area, offered those unusual mountains that rise suddenly vertical like stellagmites, an obvious reason for so many artist-inspired renditions. Snake wine is sold on board, and on unavoidable display is a bottle of the stuff, complete with an entire snake in the bottle. It was a popular purchase for which I had no desire. When I think of it, I unconsciously swallow hard.

Guangzhou, formerly Canton, was our last stop in Mainland China. It will be remembered as the only place where the people in this group enjoyed the food. The reason? Cantonese kitchen, the style to which most Americans are accustomed. I admit, I, too, was happiest with the menu there.

Then came the railroad experience. We were ushered by our guide to the crowded railroad station where the train was to take us to Kowloon, in Hong Kong, a ride of a few hours without a guide.

All our luggage was accounted for, ticketed and taken to a place where I hoped it would somehow accompany us. The seats were reserved and all together. My printed instructions from the travel company stated that when we arrived in Hong Kong, the group was to go up on the escalator from the platform and exit to the right when they reached the terminal upstairs. I was to go to the left to claim everyone's luggage from whoever was handling it. It sounded a little less than distinct, but all previous written instructions had worked, so I assumed this would, as well.

When the train was nearing our destination, I worried that we would miss our stop, not being certain that Kowloon was the end of the line. There were several stops within a few minutes of each other, and each time I fretted that we might be at the end. Finally Kowloon was where we landed.

Getting off onto the platform, we found ourselves with what seemed like a city's population. The platform was so crowded it was impossible to keep everyone together. I had already explained that they were to go one way at the top, I another. I assured the group I would eventually find them in the waiting room but that I did not have any idea of the time that would take. To add more frustration, the gates to the escalator were closed after a certain number of people had gone through. No one told us it was to stagger the crowd. In the time it took to reopen the gates, many people became nervous and even frantic. The gates opened, and a swarm went through, and the gates closed once more. The time it took for all to get onto the escalator seemed endless. People traveling together and finding themselves temporarily separated were rightfully worried. Eventually, all got through, but the scene was something like a refugee scene from "The Last Train From Madrid", back in the thirties.

When I exited left, as per prescription at the end of the escalator ride, I found myself in a maze of strewn luggage. The thirty-plus suitcases from my group were not in any order; they were not together on one baggage cart. The assistance I depended upon was in the form of one small, disabled Chinese man with a speech impediment and face and body dripping with perspiration. He was the sole attendant responsible for the dozens and dozens of tagged, but not organized, suitcases. He obligingly offered assistance but had another group before mine. I sorrowfully began to pull off my group's individual bags from the various carts that held them, quickly equaling the porter's perspiration state.

I first had to spot the identifying tags, and then pull off each heavy piece and slide it to one spot against a wall in order to establish some kind of order. Bags had been piled four and five high. To remove a bag on the bottom meant I had to remove all those above it first. To handle thirty bags meant I had to handle a hundred. I had had a quintuple heart by-pass a few years earlier. I rarely thought about it, but it was on my mind at this point, certainly. I also had been hospitalized with chronic back trouble, from which I suffered off and on, and which was a major incentive for my having retired. I feared I could not get out of this situation without one of those two problems returning to ruin me for good. I feared panic.

In what seemed like two hours, but which was something less than one, this little handicapped man and I assembled all those bags, which I checked and re-checked. We got them onto two huge airport wagons and entered the terminal waiting room, where smiles of relief greeted us in the persons of my group and our Hong Kong guide, who said the bags should all have been together on one wagon from the start because they were to have been arranged according to their name tags. To be told there is an express train to your destination after you have climbed eighteen mountains does not comfort.

I had loved the China experience and all things about it. I had wanted that strange and different world. But after minutes in Hong Kong I was thrilled at the newness, the modernity, the cleanliness–ah, the cleanliness–the air conditioning, hearing English, seeing buildings that were reminiscent of home, seeing signs like *PIZZA HUT* and *MC DONALD'S*.

The next day was a guided tour of all that everyone tours to see in Hong

Kong, including Victoria Point and Stanley Market, and then there were to be two days at leisure, the first such days on this two weeks-plus trip. I was so happy. It meant I could be alone, with no responsibility, no counting, no checking. I planned to eat in each of the fast-food places and just stroll on my own, go to my huge Omni hotel room early each evening and relax. The trip had been a strain, no doubt about it. And the luggage problem at the station had just about done me in. I spent my free times walking the crowded shopping streets of Kowloon instead of sightseeing, which I ordinarily would be wont to do. I found myself buying lots of clothing because of the great buys in shirts and silks. I ate alone most of the time, but I did learn of a popular American-type restaurant called *JIMMY'S KITCHEN*, a few blocks from the hotel. I arranged a farewell dinner for the group, which was greatly appreciated by them and myself.

The trip came to an end, and I was thrilled to get home. Most of the people in the group blur now in my memory, but not Gail. She was coarse throughout the trip, and I found myself spending time trying to avoid her. People in the group understood her attempts to latch on to me, and they were helpful about inviting me to sit with them at mealtimes, to help me escape her company. She had a habit of calling to me from great distances to get my attention. She also tried to sit with me on the bus at all times. I remembered the company's request that I give her the red carpet treatment because she was a travel agent, but the strain was painful. It felt as though I always had to peel her off. Other than a pretty good sense of humor, all her characteristics were repulsive.

Later that year I repeated the trip with my own group and some of the company's, and it went without kinks, and, of course, without Gail.

The following year I had the opportunity to take another group of strangers to China, this time on a Yangtze River cruise, an extended trip. I accepted easily and took thirty-three strangers back to China. The cruise alone gave a totally different slant.

I lucked out in having a cabin on the top deck. Each cabin had its own section of deck outside, so when the boat was cruising and the group was not together, I spent time sitting out there, reading and watching the intriguing scenery, paying attention to the sailing through the famous Three Gorges, constantly amazed at the brown, murky water.

On the way to boarding the ship, our young, bright guide had asked if we would like to visit a family who lived in the countryside on the way. The group unanimously accepted the offer with eagerness. The home was less than a hovel, consisting of two small, dank rooms with earth and concrete floors, one for the family and one for their pigs. The one electric bulb, reminding me of the one bulb in the home in Nepal, gave insufficient light, obviously, and the idea that the half-dozen family members shared one sleeping bed-of-sorts was painfully depressing. The floor was permanently wet, and the stench from the pigs was sickening. Like others, I was unable to breathe and had to exit. The family smiled sweet smiles. As usual, I thought of well-to-do families back home that do not smile in their posh palaces.

One woman in the group, a flashy blonde with tremendous boobs and lots of makeup and jewelry, who tooth-picked her teeth more than anyone I ever knew, kept recalling the scene, and, when she didn't like some of the food from the ever-present lazy-Susan on the table, would laughingly refer to it as pig-floor food. Somehow it was funny. Amazingly, the look and taste of some of the looser-consistency food began to recall the scene because of her association.

Going through the huge locks on the river, having been told about the coming dam building, seeing villages which would, in the next decade, become inundated and lost forever, the cruise became more than sight-seeing and, rather, a deep cultural/historical lesson.

One side trip was especially memorable to me. The boat docked, and we all disembarked and immediately boarded a dinosaur of a bus that would take us on a two-hour ride through mountainous territory. The bus was older than any I had ever seen. The driver sped through areas that seemed too treacherous for speed. He took dangerous curves like a roller coaster, and every time we descended he shut off the engine and coasted. The condition of the roads was pathetic, and I could not imagine we would arrive wherever we would arrive, safely. There were non-stop gasps and screeches, but on we flew. At no time was there a letup in the recklessness of the driving, but it apparently was standard procedure, and I tried to keep my Adam's Apple down while I prayed for deliverance.

Finally we arrived at a peak of a mountain. We all looked at our watches to assure ourselves that it really was two hours of this dragon coaster ride that we had survived. Then we faced a steep and long descent by an irregular, narrow and dangerous foot path. Runners were available for anyone who preferred a litter in which to be carried at high speed by barefooted carriers. Those with walking difficulties did opt for that. The rest, myself included, proceeded to descend with our guide. In areas the narrow path was muddy, then stony, then grassy, then pebbly. But we did all reach the bottom without incident. At the bottom we came upon the Shennong River, a narrow, clear stream sided by tall mountains, as if the river had cut through. Boats awaited us. They were about thirty feet in length, but only about six feet wide. Three, possibly four people could sit in one seat, and there were four or five seats per boat. We all fit into two boats, tightly packed. Four barefooted men in very primitive dress manned the boat, one steering, one guiding, one poling and one ruddering. As we passed through narrow sections of stone mountains, the poler would sink the point of his twenty-foot pole into an awaiting niche in the stone and shove the rapidly moving boat on its course. The guide tried to explain history and method as we shot through. In all places, the shallow water revealed crystal clear views of the pebbly river bed, a sharp contrast to the yellow-brown opacity of the raging Yangtse. Here and there, in wider areas, we noted groups of four natives hauling similar boats back to the direction from which we started. The guide explained that our ride down was two hours long, including one stop, but that to return the boats, against the current, took eight walking hours, for there was no other way to reverse the route. I hastily calculated what that meant in terms of manpower and wages. Each group of men could do this trip, then, only once a day, two hours down, eight hours back, with some added time between. Eight hours of walking the boat back against the flow of water. I thought of the expression "coolie labor." None of these men seemed unhappy, but what kind of a life was that, and how long would one do it? I scanned their faces for hints of age, but I could read nothing. I thought of the men who carried the people down from the top of the mountain, earlier. These people spend their lives, barefooted, carrying people and boats, day after day.

I looked at the boat itself. It was brutally heavy. At the end of the trip, these four men per boat had then to reverse direction and then haul the boat, thirty feet of it, sometimes on the water, sometimes on their shoulders. At times they sang. Was that to lift their spirits? This was slavery to me. I felt guilty to be their burden, though I realized I provided their livelihood. The physical experience was exhilarating and thrilling, but I also felt miserable pangs of guilt.

Halfway along this journey through untouched nature was an obligatory stop. In the middle of all this waited a tourist stop. I hesitate to use the famous words, "Tourist Trap." It was not a trap. But there were wares to buy and refreshments to be had. I made a couple of purchases because I was unable to ignore the people. They did not press; I just could not turn away.

At the end of the river, where it emptied into the Yangtse, our big Yangtse boat was already at the pier, waiting for us. Upon returning to my cabin, I meditated about the past few hours' experience. It had all been especially thrilling and memorable, but it caused me to be quite contemplative for the remainder of the day.

We completed our Yangtse River cruise at Wuhan, where we encountered our only rain. I was left with a dismal impression, and then we left for Guangzhou to catch the train again for Hong Kong. This time our luggage was handled correctly. With the free time in Hong Kong, I had decided this time to venture into exotic Macau, and on into Zhongshan. Almost the entire group asked to join me, so I had company, which was good. It was a full-day excursion.

Macau was all too brief, and there was no time for the illusion of the mystery and intrigue Macau had provided in movies. The visit to Zhongshan consisted of little more than a tour of the estate of Sun Yat Sen, at which point we were more aware of the intense humidity. I remember being so conscious of the women's hair stuck to their faces and necks. A very proper young Chinese college man was our guide. He was the most refined of all the guides we had seen in China. I hoped the tour members would tip him well, because he obviously didn't get the tourism that the more popular parts of the country did. He showed off his country with pride, though there was little in this area to impress, and when he offered to take us to see a private dwelling, I could think only of the family that shared its two rooms with pigs.

A pleasant surprise was that he took us to a clean, presentable house which even boasted a television. It was an old lady who welcomed us to her tiny but immaculate home. It seemed to have just one large room, but she was justifiably proud of it. Again I thought of the happiness displayed by the owner, when back at home it would have been too humble to exhibit.

When the bus returned us to the Zhongshan dock, I paid attention to the large number of Chinese people who took the ferry from there to Macao to buy economy-sized packages of toilet paper as if they were walking to the corner store for the newspaper.

Back in the Omni in Hong Kong, I was introduced to an American girl who was a guide from the same company as the one that ran my trip. They were to leave the next day for home, just as we were, although they had taken a different trip from ours.

"I'm leaving on a flight two hours before my group's," she said.

"How can that be?" I asked. "Don't you travel with them the whole way?"

"That's the way it was booked," she answered.

Immediately I recalled how difficult it had been for me even to *find* my group in the airport in Tokyo. Each tour member had been given a badge from the company, as well as a flight bag. And they had been told to look for me. I had walked all around the circular waiting room, wearing my badge, carrying my flight bag, holding a company sign, hoping these strangers would call out to me. Instead I had had to approach people, sitting with their flight bags out of sight, and ask them if they were looking for Bob Globerman. Almost none of them, for some reason, had even tried. I don't know where the communication system was. When I found each of them in my own probing way, they generally asked, "How did you know it was me?"

My reply was constant: "I didn't know. I had to keep asking anyone who looked like he might be going to China, whatever that means."

And that never seemed strange to them.

At any rate, now I was hearing that this young lady was just leaving her group who somehow would make their own way back.

"I see you're leading a group," said an elderly man in her group. "We have no one to get us through the airport. Will you take us?"

There were many elderly people with the man, all looking somewhat helpless, and it can be, indeed, a somewhat frightening prospect to get through an airport that is foreign, strange and crowded. They were like children who had just lost their teacher in the museum.

"Could you?" asked the guide. "Would you?"

"Sure," I answered. "How many of you are there?"

"Thirty-six," answered the guide.

"Holy smoke!" I responded. "I have thirty-*three*! That's sixty-nine people! And I don't even know yours!"

"Please!" cried a few of the tourists.

I arranged with their driver to coordinate leaving the hotel with my own bus, and we set out for the airport.

There were unusually large crowds of people at the entrance, and I learned immediately that the last plane that arrived had slid off the runway, blocking all flights in and out. The plane was there with one wing tipped into the water. All flights would be delayed. The other guide had taken the last flight out. She will never know her luck. Now I was stranded with sixty-nine people.

Everything was shut down. The luggage could not be processed. Lines to the check-ins, after two hours of waiting in them, became meaningless. There was no word on the length of the delays, only that there would be delays. Many people showed signs of panic: My children won't know what happened.–The limo is to meet me in L.A.!–What happens with my connecting flight?–What'll we do with our bags?–I can't carry this around!–What do we do now?–Can we get something to eat?–How do we all stay together?–This is ridiculous!–We should sue someone!

Thousands of people were filling the terminal, all wanting to get out. The lines that led to the check-in counters began to blur. The people and luggage caused such density there was no way to walk or move in any pattern. How could I direct sixty-nine people?! Monitors gave no informational help. There were only rumors hinting at the ever-lengthening waits. Rumors floated about the mis-landed plane. Were there casualties? Would it be safe to take off? Will there be landings? Will there be departures? Are they telling the truth? Why aren't there announcements?

Not knowing what else to do, I suggested that the people in my now-two groups leave their luggage with me in the center of the terminal. There obviously were no other groups of that size. I told them to circle their bags around me and go get something to eat and make their obligatory phone calls. I did suggest that someone come eventually to relieve me. Surrounded with close to a hundred suitcases and carry-ons, I remained in the center of this nightmare, wondering if logic would ever enter the scene. There were no seats of any kind in this huge waiting area, and all around, people were smoking in spite of the no-smoking rules.

The time until enough of these two groups returned to relieve me seemed endless. I wanted to get word to my faithful, waiting Regina at home. It was a few hours before there were enough returnees of the two groups to warrant my leaving to look for a phone. The latest word was that it would be twelve hours before we could hope to depart. I constantly thought of the luck of the guide who had taken the earlier flight, the last one to get out.

I located the telephones. There were four in a row, each with a waiting line of at least thirty people. I automatically began to calculate: if each person took just five minutes— five times thirty is a hundred fifty minutes–two and a half hours–they'll take more than five minutes–that's getting up to three hours–sheez!

As the line inched toward the phone, I kept praying that the phone would not go out of order, which would be typical of my fate. The woman in front of me was Japanese. When she moved up to the phone, she signaled to the other lines, and one Japanese from each line, each near the front in their prospective lines, moved out of their lines and came to her. I did not realize what was happening at first. When the woman at the phone in my line finished her call, she made another and another and then had each of the three others come to the phone to make their calls. The four of them, one in each line, had planned that whichever one reached a phone first would make the calls for all the others. I lost it. After hours in line, I had to shout, "How could you do this?" After hours in line, to be faced now with the equivalent of a dozen more people! The four looked at me for less than a second and totally ignored me. I am sure they understood what my anger was, but they never showed whether or not they even spoke English. But they knew exactly what they were doing and were prepared for objections. The people in line behind me took up the cause more agitatedly than I, so there was nothing more I needed to do, and nothing mattered to the perpetrators anyway. Would damning them damn them? I learned new meaning for boiling blood.

When I finally got through to Regina, I told her I would get back to her from L.A. Our take-off from Hong Kong would be at least thirteen hours late, and there was no way I could get to a phone later. Add another half-day for flight time and start calling the airlines at that point to get something of an approximation. That was the best I could offer. Since the world never created anyone more understanding than Regina, my worry for her sake was over; it was only my own exasperation I had to deal with.

I pacified the waiting groups as much as I could, and as much as *they* could, they were understanding. About twenty-four hours after arriving at the Hong Kong airport, we landed in L.A., where our processing was expedited by understanding airport personnel who did everything possible to assuage our troubles, fully aware of what everyone had experienced. Catching the last lap of the journey, the flight from L.A. to New York seemed like a blessing. A trip to China takes about an entire day from New York, what with flights, connections, and waits. To add all this travail (how close travail is to travel, sometimes) to the return left blotches on the memory of the beautiful experience. But–once home, the trip remains and the trials fade. Pretty much.

5

CAPE MAY OR MAY NOT

G ive me a few pages to get into this one.

One very special aspect of Globetrottours has been the weekend trips. They all ran from Friday at 7:30 in the morning, when we departed, till Sunday at seven in the evening, when we returned. They all took place within three to four hours driving time from Westchester County, New York.

The choice places were Boston, Massachusetts; Newport, Rhode Island; the Gold Coast of Long Island; Brandywine Country, overlapping Pennsylvania and Delaware; Philadelphia, Pennsylvania; and Cape May, New Jersey. Each place had its own special draw, but the attractions were mainly museums and mansions. In Boston, it was the Museum of Fine Arts and the Isabella Stewart Gardner Museum, plus all the colorful areas such as Newberry Street, Faneuil Hall and Quincy Market, and the Historic Trail.

In Newport it was mainly the Millionaires' Mansions, from the Breakers and Marble House through Astor's Beechwood and Belcourt Castle to Hammersmith Farm.

The Gold Coast of Long Island has its share of mansions, with Westbury Gardens, Coe Hall, Sagamore and the Vanderbilt Estate.

Brandywine's attractions were the DuPont Museums, Winterthur, Nemours, Hagley Mills, Longwood Gardens and the Brandywine Museum, housing so much of the Wyeths' works.

Philadelphia was the big art attraction, with the Museum of Fine Arts, the

Pennsylvania Academy of Fine Art, the art collection at the University of Pennsylvania, and the Barnes Collection, as well as the historic district with all its Americana.

All those restored and preserved Victorian houses in the landmark town of Cape May provided the interest in that special place on the coast.

Of course, I'm leaving out a million other places we visited, but at least you get a framework of the weekend itinerary.

The motorcoach seats forty-seven, and we never had an empty seat. Rather, we had waiting lists. Sign-ups for these trips were quick because word got around that they were quickly filled. If someone had to drop out at the last minute (though there was a deadline after which payments could not be refunded) rarely were we unable to fill the spot and return the original person's money. Besides, even if I couldn't fill the spot, I'd have returned the money as long as I could talk the suppliers into returning it to me, and most times I was persuasive.

The people arrived at the place of departure, where they could leave their cars for the weekend, and the joy began before the bus took off. The trips were so popular and so well attended by repeaters that most people knew each other as soon as they set foot onto the parking lot. The average person took almost every weekend trip, had the routine down pat, and got excited to see someone from a previous trip. As they arrived they kissed not only Regina and me but, often, someone they'd met on an earlier trip.

For some, the drive from home to the spot we left from was a hour. To get there in plenty of time for departure meant having to rise early that morning. Regina and I brought refreshments to add some cheer to the ride, though the cheer was there with the passengers themselves. You could sense that they knew they'd have a good time, and the chatter was bright and merry. Their anticipation was a happy form of exhilaration.

The typical itinerary was as follows: Upon arrival we stopped at our first site. It sounds mechanical to say everything was timed, but there is no other way to assure visits to everything I had planned. Appointments were made with much thought to the logical amount of time needed to get to and see everything in a packed schedule.

After our first stop, it was generally time for lunch. Two more site visits followed, and then we checked into our hotel. In every case but one, the hotel was part of the appeal. We almost always had hotels that had some special charm.

On the first evening, we likely had dinner in the hotel because the day had been long and tiring, and to add to the traveling by going out somewhere would have been a bit too much. So ended Friday.

On Saturday the routine was similar, in that we visited at least three sites, for about an hour and a half each. When a museum is one of the sites, the visit is longer, but even then there seems not to be enough time, of course. And there must always be some time built into the schedule for people to shop when we are in a unique place, as all these places are.

Breakfast is in the hotel, lunch is wherever we happen to be, and then Saturday dinner is a special treat. It might be dinner in an off-beat restaurant and then theater; it might be dinner-theater; once we had a murder-mystery dinner evening in the fabulous Belcourt Castle in Newport; it might be dinner on board a boat, such as The Spirit of Philadelphia, replete with Broadway entertainment. Whatever the case is, Saturday is the day that ends with a special evening.

Sunday breakfast is again in the hotel, after which we check out and visit our first site. The second site follows, as often as possible at a place handy for lunch afterwards. The last site is located where browsing and shopping can wind down the day, and then we're off for home.

Working out the details is as time-consuming as for the foreign trips. After deciding on a hotel for a particular weekend, I call the first site and make a reservation for ten A.M. Then I call the restaurant where we will have lunch at noon. Next is the second site for the day, say two o'clock. When I call the third site and request a reservation for four o'clock, they tell me they're booked for four, but they can take us at ten. So I have to call the first place back and see if I can switch the two times.

The first place says that's the only time they have for that day; can we make it on Saturday?

Well, there is a logical order in visiting. I might, for example, want to visit historic places important in their chronological order, or I might want places that are geographically close to each other to avoid back-tracking and wasting travel time. All this means that the scheduling has to be worked out with order, logic and practicality. To schedule nine or ten sites for one weekend can take a week of telephoning because one cannot get a definite answer on the spot in every case. Sometimes I have to call back; sometimes I have to wait to be called. It is often exasperating because I worry that we will not be able to schedule every place I want to include. However, the track record is good. Once the hotel, restaurants and sites have confirmed our appointments, each one being handled individually, I am ready to make up the flyer and send it out.

There have been times when I used a travel service to coordinate all this, but it raised the cost, and often the companies wanted to provide a step-on guide, which is unnecessary and, more often than not, a waste in that the guide has too often made goofs, such as getting us lost, and not appealing to the group because we haven't been lucky enough to get winners. So the service saves me the time and effort in making all the appointments, but then we encounter problems on site that we don't have otherwise. The result is that our trips have been more successful when I have done the entire thing step by step, alone.

Well, my few pages of introduction are up, and it's time to get to Cape May.

Regina and I were invited as guests of a famous old hotel to come for what is known in the business as a "site inspection". That means you go and stay at a hotel that will house the group, where, in turn, you visit a number of guest rooms and tour the facility, seeing the dining room, public rooms and the like. During your stay, you take the time to visit the sites to which the group will be taken.

It was our first visit to Cape May, a place we had long talked of, if only for ourselves. We were thoroughly impressed with the entire town and everything it had to offer. Our stay at the hotel was most enjoyable, but on our first night there, there was a terrible thunderstorm. It became so bad, electrical power in the hotel was lost and somehow, possibly because of a thunderbolt, the fire alarm went off.

It was the Saturday night of the Firemen's Ball, and the Fire Department arrived, not in firemen's garb, but in tuxedos. The streets were flooded, and from the veranda we watched the firemen wade across the street in high rubber boots. The situation was taken in hand, no one was terribly excited, and the evening ended with happy talk. We made a reservation for a couple of months later, and I set about creating the itinerary.

As usual, the trip sold out in record time, and we looked forward to taking the group.

At the beginning of the week preceding the weekend of that trip, there were warnings of an approaching formidable storm. As the week progressed, the warnings got more severe. On Thursday, I had to make a decision as to whether we could embark on the trip the next morning. There was no way I could wait until morning, because there would not be time to alert everyone at the last minute. I had never been faced with this kind of problem.

Having been glued to all radio and TV weather reports, and imagining getting down to Cape May and becoming stranded in bad weather, on Thursday I cancelled the trip. On Friday Hurricane Hugo struck.

Because the owners of the hotel foresaw no problem, they would not refund a five hundred dollar deposit. I understood that our group would have made up the largest portion of their guest occupancy, and maybe chances are that the hotel people would have been able to rent those rooms if they had not been reserved for us. So I made the big decision—not in my favor. The loss was not passed on to the travelers. I swallowed it.

The next season I made the same reservation, this time at a different location, a hotel facing the ocean. The trip went without a hitch, providing everyone with a new favorite spot. Before the trip ended, there were requests to return during another season.

Cape May became a place to which we returned rather regularly, almost yearly. Then came our last trip there. It was the weekend of Halloween.

Because the hotel was planning its own Halloween masquerade for Saturday night, October 31, we used Friday for our special dinner, which was held in a Victorian mansion, and after which the waiters and waitresses became performers in an old-time Western mystery performance, providing many laughs for their receptive audience. Having had our usual tours of Mansions-cum-Bed-and-Breakfasts, as well as our touring through that warm and inviting coastal town, everyone got set for the after-dinner masquerade on Saturday.

As is always the case, most of the passengers on this trip were women. And as always, everyone was in excellent spirits. Each of these weekend trips included a number of teachers Regina and I have known for years. Some of them had even taught our own children. On every trip they have been the life of the party, and when people called in their reservations, many asked if "those teachers" will be there.

As has happened in the past, three shared a triple room, and anyone near their room could expect to hear constant laughter.

Although I had not been informed ahead of time, the hotel was undergoing renovations due to new ownership. One of the unattended problems was that an occasional door did not lock properly. The three teachers were concerned about that because the rooms did open to fairly public passageways. They and I tried to fix the lock, but it did not hold. We summoned hotel help, but even the handyman did not fix it satisfactorily. The young women decided they would merely barricade the door from the inside when they turned in for the night. And they set about working with their costumes.

It happened that that night was also the night to turn the clocks back for Daylight Saving Time. I had to be sure to tell the desk, because I didn't want our appointment schedule to get fouled up on Sunday, especially because we were to have an appealing boat ride.

The crowd appeared for the masquerade with lots of good sports in every kind of costume. The most outlandish costumes were worn by the most unlikely people. The more staid the person, the more outrageous the outfit, it seemed. The hotel provided music; many danced; many sat and enjoyed watching others; and prizes were passed out for the best costumes. By midnight most people worked their way back to their rooms and went to bed.

At two in the morning a fierce storm erupted. "What is this with Cape May?", I wondered. As on our first visit in the first hotel, the alarm went off. So did the electricity. Not knowing what was happening, people wanted to leave their rooms. From their terraces they could see the ocean water crashing, but there was no way to find out what was wrong in this darkened hotel. In addition, the air conditioning had been turned off for the season, and the lack of air was stifling.

The three teachers had reason to panic. They had barricaded their door and now had to struggle in the dark to remove their handiwork in order to get out. The alarm rang, the sea crashed, everything rattled. Trying to call the desk was futile. We were not the only guests in the hotel, and with everyone trying to find out if there was imminent danger, the scene was close to pandemonium.

Many appeared in the lobby, having walked down the stairs because the elevator was not working. Fortunately no one was caught in the elevator. There were no good explanations as to why the alarm had gone off or even what caused the power failure. Most people took the incident in stride and, more or less, laughed at it.

Of course, in the morning, the desk did not give the correct wake-up call, having failed to acknowledge the time change, in spite of my having pointed it out the night before. There was much confusion. The new owner of the hotel offered many apologies for all the things that had gone wrong, mainly the possible danger for the three teachers having had to barricade themselves in. The possible negative consequences were frightening. Fortunately, the women were great sports and were able to joke about it afterwards, making the entire episode more fun and more exciting than just the regular weekend would have been. One of them, the group's humorist anyway, wrote a hilarious account of the entire weekend and not only read it aloud on the bus on the way home, but sent copies to the others on the trip. Our morning boat ride obviously had to be cancelled, but people were happy to have the time to shop.

Trips are memorable because of the sites you visit and what you learn. You take a particular trip because you're interested in learning about the places listed in the itinerary. There are the additional pleasures of the hotels and restaurants, the exploring, the browsing, the shopping and the special purchases you bring back. Extra added pleasures are the good people you meet and travel with, often a serendipity of its own. When, in addition to these factors, circumstances happen that make the unexpected as exciting as the trip, it's cream on the cake. When friends meet sometime afterwards and talk of the good times on the trips, the most colorful parts of their memories are the offbeat, unexpected adventures that no planning can provide. The person who does not make the best of it and enjoy it for what it is is in the tiny minority. Good sportsmanship is a vital ingredient. It's a rare person who does not realize that the best laid plans of mice and men . . . The necessary spontaneity is a gift of life.

The return trip on Sunday night has its own flavor. Everyone's exhausted because the three days have been so full. But there is still an exhilaration. Some chatter, some reminisce, some sleep, but all have a feeling of fullness. And without exception, on every trip home the question arises: "Bob, where are we going next? What trips do you have planned? How about . . . ?"

When the bus deposits us where the people had left their cars, there are hugs and kisses and the warmest feelings. Most of the people come from neighboring towns and cities, and the end of the trips does not mean the end of the relationships. Sometimes we bump into these friends, sometimes they call. Knowing that I have retired, a common question is "If you ever decide to lead another trip . . . " or "Couldn't you do just one more?" It's flattering, heartwarming, endearing, touching. However, all good things must come to an end. It's just that whenever anyone mentions any of the weekend places, I am unable to separate the places from the people on the trips. I automatically see them as reminders of the wonderful people who made all those weekends wonderful.

6

A FEW BUMPS

Wilderstein is an interesting old Queen Anne house in the Hudson Valley, opened to tourism a good part of the year. On a Sunday in spring, after visiting two other mansions in the area and stopping for lunch, our motorcoach made its way into the lane that leads to the building's porte cochere. Though the driveway went through the porte cochere, it was not open for traffic due to construction scaffolding supporting its roof. The people were let off in the driveway, and the driver pulled the huge vehicle onto the lawn to the side of the entrance.

Immediately the motorcoach began to sink into the clay-bodied lawn. The passengers turned to see the wheels imbedded in mud up to their rims. Since we had an appointment as the last group of the day for a house tour, I took care of the arrangements at the entrance and went back to the bus. A couple of men in the group were good enough to accompany me as the remainder of the group entered for their tour. With the driver, the men and I went in search of some wood or brush to place under the rear wheels for traction. We found very little, but what we did find we placed beneath the more sunken of the two rear wheels. We called to the driver to try to rock the bus out of its pit. One revolution of the wheels and the wood went flying. The situation was hopeless. The coach was pathetically stuck in sheer mud.

The driver suggested the men and I join the group inside while he used the coach's phone to locate a towing company, no small task considering that this was a Sunday and the vehicle in distress was a huge 48-passenger monster.

The tour was as interesting as always, but, as always, it was over in less than an hour, and a rescue unit had not yet been located. The docents inside Wilderstein were at a loss for what to do with us.

Wilderstein was inhabited by its last owner, Margaret "Daisy" Suckley, a cousin of Franklin Delano Roosevelt. She was in her late nineties, and, at the time, there was no talk of the relationship between the two cousins—only the story that she had been the one who had given the former president his dog Fala.

I had seen Ms. Suckley once before on a previous visit, but only from a distance. The tiny woman (she was less than five feet tall) appeared now in the background, standing in her walker, gazing out at us through thick lenses, wearing a huge smile. In a moment's time, after she exchanged some words with the bewildered guides, we were informed that she was inviting us to enjoy tea and cookies after making ourselves at home. The transportation problem was quickly forgotten by everyone except those who had to notify friends and family about the delay. The phone was made available, and everyone settled in on the veranda and an enclosed porch, as two women guides brought out trays of cookies and pots of tea.

I went out to check with the driver who, so far, had not been able to contact a towing company equipped to haul such a load. Upon my return, I noticed the smiling Ms. Suckley standing in the hallway. She had been talking a bit to various members of the group, something she did not normally do, remaining out of sight during touring times. There was an arrangement with the Wilderstein Preservation Group that she live in the house the remainder of her days, with the necessary personal and health care as well as care of the home, something it definitely needed. Upon her death, the preservation group would take over the running of Wilderstein as a private property.

This unusual event, detained guests, was something of a serendipity all around. The group felt it was a one-time, chance, unexpected treat that outshown the visit; Ms. Suckley seemed to feel likewise in return, openly happy with the spontaneity of the turn of events.

I leaned to her and said, "The house is wonderful, and so is your hospitality, but the best part of it all is meeting you."

She crooked her finger, signaling me to bend closer, and said, "Thank you. Nobody ever said that to me." I found that hard to believe. She smiled with a twinkle. What a sweetheart. Soon she retired to her quarters upstairs.

Three hours after our arrival, the driver informed us that help was on its way. He had called fourteen towing companies in three states before he could get proper help. An outfit arrived and hauled the stuck bus out of its claypit. I have no idea who took care of the repair of the lawn, which was deeply rutted and ruined. But the delayed ride home disturbed no one, because everyone was satisfied with the extra treat of having met Daisy Suckley.

About a year later I read in the newspapers of her passing, and eventually out came the book and media data that told of her closer-than-we-had-been-led-to-believe relationship with F.D.R. It bothered me to read all that, but I was pleased that Ms. Suckley was not around to know about it. The dear lady was almost a hundred. How good that she was spared, at least, the notorious gossip.

On another one-day bus trip in the Hudson Valley, with another bus company and another driver, we were gathered in the parking lot when the driver informed us he had to go and get gas, not having had time before our appointed meeting. He returned shortly, announced that this was his first day with the company, and off we went.

Twenty minutes under way, a few people in the rear of the bus, which was filled this time with senior citizens, complained that there was a peculiar odor. Shortly after, they stated that something was dripping in the back. The driver stopped the bus, walked to the back inside, then went outside, and returned to say he found nothing. We proceeded on our way.

By the time we were half an hour from our point of departure, people toward the rear of the bus complained about fumes and odor. I had the driver pull the bus off the road and asked the people to exit and move away from the bus. I had no idea what might be wrong, but fearing the worst, I wanted to take no chances.

When the first visit of a four-visit trip is delayed, obviously the rest of the itinerary dominoes. I had to call place number one, the most distant of all, to warn them of the delay; they were opening only for this group. But we were nowhere near a phone. The driver could not call outside from this bus; he could only call the office. I asked him to have the office call ahead to warn of our plight.

Through some strange quirk of fate that defies odds, a car that was not far behind us pulled over to find out what our problem was; its driver worked for the bus company and was on his way home. When he announced that, I almost kissed the ground in disbelief/relief. He went with the bus driver to the rear of the bus, examining. In the meantime, they alerted the company to send a replacement bus.

I worried about the possible anger of the group in view of their scheduled touring being ruined. The people I heard from assured me that this all just added to the sense of adventure. Not to worry.

In some time, the driver informed us that he had apparently pumped the gas into the air conditioning system. He was embarrassed, flustered, sheepish, ashamed and all the obvious. The average comment was, "Well, I would think he *would* be."

Sooner than I would have expected, the replacement bus arrived, and we were scooted off with a new driver and an untroubled bus, leaving the original bus and driver waiting for rescue.

At the first available phone, I left the bus to call our first stop. Though dismayed, the director of our visit to Bronck House in Cocksackie proved totally helpful in accommodating us. Though willing to take all the time in the world to give us our anticipated tour of this group of houses which are a museum of generations who lived on the property in the past two centuries, it was difficult to make up so much lost time, and I had to ask this caring woman to hasten the visit just a bit. There was only so long I could push back lunch and each of the other two sites. I tried to concentrate not on what the group would be missing in a paced-up visit, but, rather, that they might not know everything was slightly abridged. It had been a two-hour drive under normal circumstances, and we had lost about an hour through the mishap. The seniors were grateful for the caring, and they were kind in their acceptance. As I called each of the remaining sites and explained to the directors and then to the group what had to happen, I felt such appreciation at everyone's cooperation.

I was grateful for the end of the day and the safe (and not-too-late) return.

1991 was the year of the Gulf War. I had thirty-four reservations for a trip to Spain which would depart on February 15. As ticketing is generally done thirty days in advance, January 15 was the day I was to make the airlines payment. The beginning of January was ominous, with negative reports about the Desert Storm situation.

On January 14 Iberia Airlines informed me that they were going to add a surcharge of fifty dollars per person for our flights.

"In view of the world situation, I'm afraid of people dropping out of the trip as it is," I told them. "If you add a surcharge now, you're going to kill it altogether for me."

"But the charge is added," they responded.

"I have thirty-four people signed up and paid for. You're talking about a difference of seventeen hundred dollars. Is it worth it to you to take a chance and lose the whole group?"

"That's the charge," they told me.

"This has already been paid for. How can you change the amount so close to departure time?"

"We're sorry, but that's how much it will be."

"Well, I can't take seventeen hundred dollars out of my pocket and pay it," I said. "And I won't ask the people to come up with the additional amount. This has never happened. These people trust me. I would never impose an additional cost. Can't you work around that, this one time? The crisis in the world will keep many people from traveling at all. Aren't you making it worse all around?"

"Well, the fares must be paid by tomorrow."

"Is there any chance at all this can be waived?" I asked.

"You have until five o'clock tomorrow."

"Is there any chance of it being waived?" I repeated.

"Well, call us by five tomorrow."

Before five the next evening, January 15, I called, saying there were people who were wavering even without the surcharge.

"The fifty dollar surcharge must be paid," I was told.

"Then cancel the whole thirty-four," I said.

The next day, January 16, the United States went to war against Iraq.

7

AIRPORTS

Somewhere in the course of writing a book there comes a time when the book writes itself. Chapter 4, which covered **INDIA** and **CHINA**, as well as Chapter 2 (**EGYPT**), gave a good deal of attention to the airport situation in those countries. So maybe it's apropos now to take time out to focus on exactly that: the airport situations. There have been plenty of those worth noting.

At the end of a marvelous February trip to Turkey, one of the most special of all countries, we had arrived at the airport as it began to snow. We were ready to leave; this was not a good time for snow. After the formalities of checking through, we waited in the terminal while a crew de-iced the plane, which we could easily see through the large, steamed-up windows of the terminal. We watched with trepidation. This was a first for me; I had never seen the process. Simultaneously, other crewmen were removing snow from the airfield, though not as quickly as it was falling. On everyone's mind was the thought that we had no assurance the plane could take off at all. Among the longest blocks of time I can remember was the time from our arrival at the airport until our eventual takeoff, more than four hours and three de-icings later. To face an unplanned extended stay in Turkey, wonderful as the country is, appealed to no one. Everyone was over-anxious to get home.

Finally the plane did depart, fortunately without incident. When we did arrive in Kennedy, half the people, including Regina and myself, did not get their luggage. We waited more than an hour, for whatever delay there might have been, only to learn that all the bags did not accompany the flight. That is always a terrible problem for anyone, less so on the return flight, however, because one is returning home to other clothing, at least. The problem does not seem lighter; one worries that the luggage will be forever lost; all those precious purchases, in addition to the clothing and other personal items inside.

I contacted the necessary airlines representative, and we all filled out the necessary claim forms. As is typical, the bags were delivered to our door by eight o'clock the next morning.

Three years later, because of requests as well as my own strong desire to return, I led another trip to Turkey, again in February.

During dinner on our last night, our hitherto guide approached me to tell me that he would not be going with us to the airport the next morning. Someone else would be taking us.

"Why?" I asked, stunned as well as concerned.

"I'm meeting an incoming group whose tour starts tomorrow."

"Why can't they get you after you've seen us off?"

"That's the way the company arranged it," he answered.

"You didn't meet us when we arrived. You met us when the touring began. Why can't it be the same with this new group?"

"I have no control over that," he said. "But there will be someone to take my place." He introduced me to a very young, pleasant *boy* who I was certain did not have the background to serve the sometimes needed service through the airport, meaning the clout to make a smooth exit through customs. Having been once burned after the incident in the Cairo airport, I was twice-shy about airport departure procedures.

Where is Amar?" I asked. Amar was a company representative I had met and liked on an earlier trip to Turkey. He was likeable, ever-smiling, spoke perfect English, and was a liaison between Turkey and its USA-based company.

A phone call got Amar to the scene. He agreed to accompany us to the airport.

Judy (See **Clientele/Client Hell**) was on that trip. Judy is that stereotype of stereotypes who goes on and on about herself and her children's accomplishments and becomes a connoisseur of a country in a two-week visit. She had never traveled with me before. When I explained that I was going for a group check-in, she asked why they couldn't all check in individually. For a reason unknown to me at the time, other than that she had been annoying here and there through the trip, and for which I have been berating myself ever since, I said okay. Mistake of a lifetime!

The procedure took two and a half hours. During that time there was usually no movement or sign of progress. Attendants at the counters invariably shifted positions or disappeared. The buck-passing was monumental. About halfway through the waiting time we were informed that the Turkish government owned exactly two of the mighty planes of which one was the plane on which we were booked. The other was out of the country somewhere. Ours was being confiscated by some governmental power for use at this time. On the substitute plane there was not room to seat my entire group in spite of the fact that I had reconfirmed our seats within the past seventy-two hours as was traditional. A dozen of our thirty could not be seated.

I've already stated that all of my groups consist mainly of women. This one was no exception. Many women travel with me because of my style of shepherding; they know they are protected; they feel safe. Now I was asked to leave a dozen people behind.

By nature, though I am an extreme worrier I am kindly-spoken and unabusive. No one has to worry too much about my temper or my language. When I could not get my point across because of the language barrier, I asked Amar to step in. This man who was so smiley-faced and jocular was reduced to a furrow-browed, sweating, panicking mass of tears. He was as helpless as the young boy substitute for our guide. A nightmare was building. Instead of my soft-spoken, gentle, cautious, supposedly diplomatic self, I heard loud cursing echoing through the area, and it was coming from me.

To everyone in authority to whom I could make myself clear, I was shouting that nobody in my group was going to stay behind, and the plane is not leaving without me; we are all to get on, goddammit!

The number of unseatables was reduced to six, but they said it could go no further. One couple and one woman agreed to take a later flight, the couple because they were told the re-routing would give them first-class or business-class accommodations and the adventure did not bother them; the woman had been ill for the past two days and the extension would give her a chance to see what she had missed because of having been confined to her hotel room.

I was standing with three of my women at the entrance to the jetway leading into the plane. One woman shakingly said, "Bob, I don't want to stay; please don't leave me."

I replied, "I'm not leaving you, and this plane is not leaving without *me!*"

I asked, as I had been asking for the past hour, that they make a loudspeaker request for anyone who would be interested in volunteer bumping. Everyone knows it's a common request of all airlines, and there is always someone who opts for the opportunity to have a serendipitous perk. They would not honor my request.

I knew the plane could not take off yet. I bolted through the jetway and into the aircraft and shouted whether anyone would volunteer to take a later plane for the obvious benefits.

Judy, already seated, said, "I should do it. I created the problem." I had no idea she was there till I heard that. But I did not accept the offer. I would not have left her any more than I would have left anyone else.

There were no takers. I rushed back to the entrance and grabbed the three waiting women and pulled them into the plane, saying, "Let them worry how to get you off." The two attendants at the entrance were dumbfounded and did not stand in the way of this madman.

It happened that there were five empty seats in the rear of the cabin. I told the women to sit there. Flight attendants said those seats were for them. I told them to do what my women were supposed to do. They said they were for any flight attendant who needed to rest during the flight; flight attendants need to sit sometimes, too. I told them they would have to work it out.

My anger was visible to everyone on that plane. I was hoarse from shouting, wet from anxiety and aware of some distant chest pains. Later, one of my good women, Jo, told me she had been worrying for me because she noticed during my fighting in the airport that I kept rubbing my sternum, something I had been unaware of.

The entire group was on the plane. I made sure that of all the times I had counted and re-counted my flock, I did it this time with extra precision and repetition. If ever I double- and triple-checked my shepherding, this was the time.

What I had not done, however, was to identify my baggage before entering. Even the three last women had had a chance to do that. All luggage had been checked in, but in that airport there is a procedure whereby each passenger identifies his bag just before entrance to the waiting room. I had not done that. I'd not had time to think about it.

When all was behind us, and we were in our homes, and even the three remainers were back, I was still on the phone with Turkish Airlines, trying to trace my suitcase. It took until the end of the week before I was able to get it. It came to my house by express, but it was badly damaged. I do not, in any way, feel that it was deliberate, but damaged it was.

The booking company replaced the suitcase, and that was fine. They were mortified to learn of the difficulty in the airport and terribly embarrassed.

At the end of the week, having brooded and feeling worn down because of the extreme aggravation and strain, I called the head of the Turkish Consulate in New York City and arranged a meeting with her. A more charming, concerned and compassionate person I never met. I told my story and was so caught up in it that my voice quivered and my eyes got wet. I had no expectation of being so emotional, and the embarrassment of it was not enjoyable.

In my presence this lovely lady called Turkish Air and then Turkey itself to inform them of this awful situation, emphasizing my love for the country and my concern for the safety and cohesion of my group. She was super. A letter of apology was sent to all the members of the group, but what more could she do?

That was really the worst of all the airports situations. To be told your entire group, for which you are responsible, cannot be on the same flight is about as frightening and threatening a situation as a tour leader can imagine.

Although this is still an "Airport" story, it requires a bit more of a lead-in. Please accept some preliminary reminiscing.

One summer I led a group on a Russian Waterways cruise. That's how it was billed–RUSSIAN WATERWAYS CRUISE. The ship was our hotel all the way through from day one to day last.

We began in St. Petersburg, in whose airport we arrived sans incident. We went through the airport routine smoothly and easily and were met, as planned, by a ship guide as soon as we reached the exit door with our luggage, and then we went swiftly to the bus that would transport us to the boat. Check-in on the boat went smoothly, and all the acclimatization proceded well.

Our first three days were non-sailing days, as we used that time to visit various and obvious spots in and around St. Petersburg. St. Petersburg was the only city in Russia I had ever visited before. My father was born in Russia, though not in St. Petersburg. I don't know if some of my fascination with the city was due in part to that, but I was definitely consumed by something that separated Russia–at least St. Petersburg, for the moment–from other places I had visited. I am extremely aware of how certain impressions I get of foreign cities are as captivating as Disney World is to children. Magical, mystical things happen to me often in foreign places. I'm careful who my audience is when I speak of it because I can get really excited by things that don't faze others. On the other hand, the reverse has proven true, as well, because quite often I don't get as thrilled as others at things that work for them. At any rate, riding through the streets of St. Petersburg, now as previously, I had an extra sense of the times of the Revolution, back in the days towards the end of the First World War. I imagined these boulevards with horse-drawn carriages rather than the vehicles of today. My mind's eye could see the families of the tsars in their furs and finery in coaches fleeting by. As we approached the Hermitage, I did not concentrate on the glorious works of art we would find inside but, instead, on the royal family that graced it. The characters, real and fictional, that had flavored my reading were almost visible.

Entering the Hermitage was unlike entering any of the countless museums which have filled my life. An artist for most of my years, it is honest to say that outside of home and school I have spent more time in museums than any other kind of place. Even movie theaters, the love of my life, have not had as much of my presence as museums, and here I was, entering the Hermitage. All the most magnificent of museums–the Louvre, the Metropolitan, the Prado, the British–all of them are thrilling to me, and all house the most glorious of works, but I am not overwhelmed by their housing. Here, in the Hermitage, I almost felt as though I wouldn't care what was hanging on the walls or standing in the galleries; pausing in the entrance, gazing up at the white and gold architecture, would have been enough. It was, first, a palace, and that's what I was seeing. I waited for royalty to appear, in regalia of generations past.

Visiting Petrodvoretz and the Catherine Palace had the same effect on me. Both are dazzling Baroque palaces that represent the ultimate in Russian luxury, personifying the era of the Czars–the Romanovs -, gaudily magnificent in the display of wealth and the most romantic images of Russian royalty at its height. The splendor of the grandest buildings of the Nineteenth Century is nowhere more pronounced than here. Concentrating on the brutal damage done by the Nazis in the forties and gazing at the restoration, I often had to shake myself back into the realization of why I was here. I was, after all, leading a group. I could not drift off into reverie.

The streets of St. Petersburg, whenever we rode through, which was several times, were bereft of people for the most part. There was always a lost, almost deserted ambience about it. And when we passed near imposing buildings in faded pastels of yellows and pinks, I realized they were in decayed conditions, at least superficially. So much cosmetic touch-up was needed. All the buildings seemed like lovely women who were not to be seen too closely because they were older and shabbier than when first noticed from across the way. Sadness overtook me. Due to the dreary cold of the winter, the buildings had been painted in these bright colors to cheer the area up. However, the colors were not bright at all.

The cruise route took us to towns we would never likely see otherwise. It was August, and there was hardly a time without some drizzle during some part of the day. We were told that there are only sixty days a year without rain in Russia. I don't know why I had never heard that before. I read up so much before each trip, yet I had not come across that, somehow. The dampness and dreariness gave an atmosphere that seemed permanently gray in feeling as well as color, and somehow all the sites seemed colored, in turn, by it.

A stop on Kizhi Island, with all its unique wooden churches with their incredible domes of glistening aspen was romantic and memorable, and proceeding from town to town after that proved that each had its special tugging claim. Lake Ladoga was unfriendly one particular day of our journey, with waters so violent that the dishes were flung from the dining tables and bottles flew off the bar. An occasional person fell because of the tossing, and many were sick. Some, including a woman in my group who had a fear of the water, became hysterical and almost impossible to calm.

The wretched conditions under which people lived in the small river towns were cause for sadness. Entering a small neighborhood store was disheartening. One of the tourists wanted to buy a package of biscuits and, after language barriers were surmounted, learned they could not be bought because there would not be enough, then, for the inhabitants. In other stores, it was pitiful to see the small amount of any item on any given shelf. If you were looking for shampoo, you might find half-a-dozen bottles in all. The shelves were sparse, the cupboard almost bare. I felt quite blue. I gazed across the dirt road to the fields opposite and saw only Tevye's land, generations back. The drabbiness of the world of *FIDDLER ON THE ROOF* was accurate. My father had not painted such an accurate picture for me.

Old women were the saddest sight. There were stops we would make at small towns in order to see the remains of Russian Orthodox churches. As soon as we disembarked and began to weave our way through forlorn paths, old women appeared, selling, or trying to sell, puny, dying flowers. It was difficult to refuse these undesirable weeds; what else had these poor souls to sell?

Moscow was a metropolis, of course, compared to all the towns we passed through to get there. And those onion domes of St. Basil's at Red Square do deserve your time for photographing them. Gum's is, yes, an interesting mall-type department store worth visiting, as is the underground train station, but the purpose in this chapter is to get you to the airport.

The ship's guide delivered us, as expected, to the entrance of Moscow's airport. He bade us all a fond adieu, and the minute he left I realized we were in bedlam. The area was as large and disorganized as any area could be. It was more jammed than Cairo's airport, which I thought was impossible to beat. Not a single sign was in English, of course, and it was virtually impossible to find an official who spoke it. Far in the distance one could make out some kind of lighted signs which indicated that that was probably where we had to be; in addition, there was some kind of gravitational pull in that direction. However, there was no logical, orderly method of getting there. People pushed and crossed in front of each other; if the thrust was from north to south, it did not prevent masses from going from east to west.

Ariadne and Allegra, whom you will meet in **Clientele/Client Hell,** were on this trip. They had a lot of baggage, and Ariadne has something of a walking problem; Allegra, her mother, was not in the best of health. In addition, Tim, another tour member, was severely handicapped, using two canes, and his wife had to manage the bags for both of them. I could not keep my group together.

When you are in a scene of near-hysteria, such as this, and you sense that there are those who are used to it, you develop a sense for finding someone who might be able to direct you. Since I must direct others, it is essential for me to get information fast. Wonderful people who've traveled with me on trip after trip, such as Jo *(Clientele/Client Hell)*, have also learned to put out antennae, and some kind of communication, unplanned, develops. Memory has blotted out the way I learned where we had to go. It was all in some vague similar direction yonder, where there were eight different signs bearing a single number from one to eight. We had to get to that point. *HOW?* was the frightening thought because I was unable to keep sight of Ariadne and her mother or Tim and his wife, let alone the rest of the group who had no walking problems when we set out.

Regina was with me on this trip. We have created our own communication system wherein, under normal circumstances, if I lead the group, she brings up the rear, or vice versa. We were unable to work it in this case. The entire world population was in this room, and I would not let my beloved out of my sight. We shuffled side by side, barring other people from separating us with our two large bags.

There was a time when I learned that some English-speaking person not from our group made it to one of the numbers overhead, only to learn she was in the wrong section. I asked anyone who seemed to understand English if I was headed correctly. Each time I asked, I was given the nod, but I needed extra assurance and kept asking someone new, until the time arrived when I was under the numbers and relieved to find the guards admitted me.

As soon as Regina and I were on "the other side," I planted my luggage with hers and asked her not to leave that spot. I wanted to go as far ahead as I could in order to see if any of the group had already gotten through to Immigration; I needed to know how many I was still looking for, behind us. At some point I was able to account for everyone, but it was close to flight time, and Ariadne and her mother, plus Tim and his wife were painfully far back in the mob.

Regina and I remained where we were until the last of our group, wet with perspiration, got through the barriers. Next was the passport control line. There were three or four booths, and the lines moved agonizingly slowly. Departure time was minutes away. I braved the possible furor of the crowd to go ahead of them to the booth, merely to ask if anything could be done to get the handicapped moved up. No one in authority spoke English. I was unable to make myself understood to anyone I needed.

When Regina and I at last reached the stamping official (a woman who never looked up) I used every form of body language as well as battered French and German to find out if the take-off would wait for the few of my group who were pitifully far back. Oh, why didn't I take Russian in college? At registration, back then, it had the shortest of lines. I know a girl who took it for that reason only.

Although there were never any answers to my questions and no one who ever seemed to care, by some miracle or strange fortune, Ariadne, Allegra and Tim and his wife materialized in our section of the final waiting area at the exact moment the gates to the field opened. I promised myself never to look a gift horse in the mouth.

Airports.

8

ON MY OWN, OR, OFF THE BEATEN TREK

No shepherd has ever watched his flock better than I watch mine. About that I am totally conscientious. My eyes are always surveying my group. If a guide is talking in a public place, my ears may be tuned to him, but my eyes are forever checking my wards. I need not wonder whether the group is aware, because I know they are. I never leave the group unattended, adults though they may be.

However, after having led most of the people several times, and having visited many places several times, there did come a few occasions where, with their approval, I left them in the care of the guide in order to explore nearby.

After a few visits to Egypt, on the last one, led by the beautiful Sahar, a total guide, we were approaching the famous site of Queen Hatshepsut's temple-tomb in the Valley of the Kings and Queens in Thebes. Certainly it is one of the most awe-inspiring sites anywhere, that magnificent edifice seen, as one approaches, in its in situ grandeur. In situ means that the entire place is carved out of the living rock. Instead of columns being created and set into place, here the space around them is cut away from the rock itself, leaving the columns as the part of the remaining area. With its long ramps, near-white columns silhouetted against the shadows they create, no one fails to be impressed. I have talked and talked about its glories in college classes as well as in public lectures.

I have a large collection of slides of everything around the world, hundreds on Egypt alone. All the slides of Hatshepsut's temple-tomb are from my own photographing. All that is, except the aerial views, which are spectacular. Those views were shot from the small mountain to the right of the temple-tomb, part of the same stone from which the building itself was hewn. I had a longing to climb that mountain and take my own shots.

Sahar anticipated a visit of close to an hour at the site. With her commanding and expert presentations, I had no doubt that the group would be glued to her. Making my explanation and receiving the group's blessing, I left them as they approached the ramp with Sahar, and I began to climb the mountain, which seemed simple enough, not rugged, not too steep.

In less than ten minutes I became aware of how steep it actually was. The tread on my sneakers did not prevent me from sliding a little, and I began to wonder if I had been wise. Of course I kept looking back toward my subject, waiting for the best views, which could only be enhanced by additional height. Maybe another fifty feet, then another fifty.

I paused to catch my breath and wipe my brow when a voice startled me enough that I almost fell backwards. I turned, and farther up the mountain was a tall figure in a galabea, the ankle-length cotton garment worn by many Egyptians. I could not see the face because the hood put it in shadow. Behind the man was an opening in the mountain, like the entrance to a cave. I had not noticed it earlier. I was not at ease. Was I about to be slaughtered? Was I back in an earlier time? Would I get out of this? I froze.

The figure approached me, towered over me, being on the up side of the mountain and tall to begin with. Then I saw a smile and realized this was a teenager. Obviously spotting an American, he spoke in broken English and from his flowing sleeve pulled out a fragment of painted ceramic or composition. It was reminiscent of wall paintings seen in tombs everywhere.

"From tomb," he said. "How much?"

Though not yet comfortable, I had to think a smile. Alone on a mountaintop or an iceberg or in a jungle, there would always be someone selling.

I shook my head. I really did not know what to offer.

A cheap two-inch flashlight dangled from my belly bag strap. He pointed to it and put his palm up.

"You want this?" I asked.

He extended the ceramic piece with one hand and held out the other.

"From tomb," he repeated. "Old."

We exchanged possessions, and he beckoned toward the cave. "You want see my house?" he smiled.

Yes, I did. But I did not feel safe. My nervousness outweighed my curiosity. I was too old to consider taking a chance. I indicated, instead, that my group was waiting for me. He retreated. I took my photos and made my way down the slippery mound. I had had enough adventure. Maybe I had better stay with the group.

The day before, we had been in Giza. On each of the trips to Giza in the past, when we arrived at the pyramids, we were told that the Great Pyramid, Khufu's (or Cheops') was not open for viewing, and each time we visited the center one, Khafre's (or Chefren's). This time, Sahar announced that we could get into Khufu's. No one was more excited than I, because I had longed to do this ever since my first visit with Regina and the kids, nearly fifteen years earlier.

The entrance is many feet above the ground, requiring that we climb up the outside quite a ways before being able to get inside. It was crowded. At the entrance, Sahar announced that she would be waiting below, and that we had about an hour and a half. She also asked us not to go down inside, only up. I realized then that there was a passageway to the left, just inside the entrance, going down, dimly lit.

It was impossible for the group to stay together. Ascending was awkward because there were areas where one had to bend over because the ceiling of the passageway was low. Doing this while climbing at a forty-five degree angle was not easy. I had remembered this from visits to Khafre's pyramid in the past. In one place there was two-way traffic. That was a little dizzying. Though the passageway was wider, the makeshift steps were difficult. However, without incident everyone made it to the top, to the room that contained the famous pharaoh's stone tomb. It was eerie, as it should be, and all my lectures came back to me. I had always gone into great detail about Egyptian history and burial rites and mummification, and the room I was in had always been illustrated by other people's slides. The broken corner of the sarcophagus was so familiar. Now I could have my own photos.

After several minutes, we all descended. When we reached the inside of the entrance, I told the person nearest me that I'd be with the group shortly. I disobeyed instructions and, with one young member of the group, began my way down the forbidden passageway. For much of the way, walking backwards was easier than frontwards. The floor slope was extremely steep, and the ceiling was so low, it meant doubling over. Walking backwards prevented falling forwards.

The lighting was minimal. There was a naked bulb about every thirty feet. On the climb down, we passed only two people coming back up. Sam, the young guy from my group, had complete faith in me and was really enjoying the adventure. But he was in his twenties and had his trust in me. I was in my sixties and should have known better and had no one in whom to place my trust. I just needed to do this. What might Sahar think, if she were to find out?

The trip down was much longer than I had anticipated, and I was concerned with using up the allotted time. And the one person who could never be late was myself. And if I was late, it would expose what I had done, where I had been.

The farther down we trod, the thinner and danker the air became. Two more people appeared, on their way back.

"Is anyone down there?" I asked.

"Not now," was the answer.

When we reached the bottom, the floor was sand. There was room to stand, but there was a solid wall eight feet ahead. At its bottom was a square opening, about three feet high. I was wearing white pants. To get through that opening meant crawling on hands and knees. We did it. But at this point I tied my handkerchief across my face because the thin air was getting stifling from the stirring up of sand.

We faced a second wall with a similar opening. Well, if we did the first, we could do the second. We did. And now we were at the end. Here was a crypt in which we could stand. It was only an irregularly shaped room with an irregular floor, containing nothing but animal droppings. Bats, I wondered?

Sam and I looked at each other, each waiting for some pearl of wisdom from this educator.

"Is that all there is?" I sang.

On our return it was necessary, of course, to crawl through those two openings again. My luck ran out just a bit. I pulled my back and felt sharp stabs of pain. I said nothing.

Ascending the long passageway was easier than the descent had been because of being able, at least, to face forward this time. However, it was still necessary to bend in half, and my back revolted. About fifty feet on the way, with Sam about ten feet ahead of me, the young fellow said he had just gotten a kink in his knee and wanted to stop for a second. Delicious words. This way I could take a rest without divulging my problem.

The rest of the climb up was slow, thankfully. A pleasure was the sense that the air was gradually becoming clearer. I mused over the small adventure which had meant a great deal to both of us. It was not just that we had done it; it was that it was something people do not do. There is always that special, sly joy in that.

I looked up at the delicious light coming in from the exit. I did not even realize how wet I was until the outside air hit me. And then, with a private smile on each of our faces, Sam and I descended on the outside in time to join the group below.

I have been to Israel so many times, I've lost track. My trips in recent years have been Holy Land tours, meaning that the subject matter is centered on Jesus and Christianity, as opposed to kibbutz life and modern Israel.

Every trip included a visit to Masada, and every ascent and descent was via the cable car. On my last trip I was determined to climb down. I did not mind ascending via the cable car, but I felt the need to do my own descent. I was sixty-two. As the Jewish saying goes, "If not now, when . . . ?"

Our guide was a man I'd used a few times before, a strong-willed, no-nonsense guy with a great sense of humor, but one who keeps a firm hand on the group. Getting assurance from the group that it was all right and that they understood my objective, an hour before they were to descend via cable car, I left them to do the same by foot, estimating the maximum time needed.

Oddly, it seemed to me, no one else was descending by foot. There were hundreds of people up there, but no one was making the descent by foot. Well, there is only one route, so I began. In the first ten minutes I did question the sensibility of my decision. The path was often steeper than I had imagined, and its surface was tricky in that pebbles slid from underfoot, and my sneakers did not always grip. There were hairpin turns with no barriers and severe drops just beyond. One small mis-step could mean a fall off the edge of the earth. And I became aware of the negative aspect of my bi-focals, something that had never before disturbed me. My dark glasses steamed quite often.

I did pass an occasional upward climber, less than half a dozen on the entire trek, but not a single soul was going the down route. I realize that while it might take more effort to climb up than down, the advantage in climbing up would be that you were leaning into the mountain. Going down left you prone to falling forward and, therefore, off.

A quarter of the way down, I turned to look at the starting point. It was a good distance away, but not nearly so far as the bottom. What would happen if I panicked and became unable to move? Would they get me out via helicopter? What would happen if I fell off altogether? What would Regina do? Why am I here? What was I out to prove? Who said I was in good enough condition to attempt this foolish caper? And then, what about my responsibility to the group?

It was typically hot and dry that day, without a movement of air. My face felt flushed, and I was extremely overheated. As is usual, I did not rest, but proceeded down, my mind cluttered with unwanted, negative thoughts I tried to displace. Heart trouble, back trouble, almost a senior citizen. What was wrong with me? Where was logic?

Damn those dangerous turns. I hadn't counted on them. At each one I could not help but think how easy it was to fall off the edge. And the pebbles that kept sliding away beneath me. They made it all so much more treacherous. The path needed a sweeping. I guess that's not something to put into the suggestion box, though. Didn't the country have the problem of people, ignorant as I, falling off? Didn't the authorities have to rescue people often? Why weren't there some guard rails? This is more dangerous than anyone had ever indicated. How did I get to be so stupid?

I think I made a small vow never to try anything like this again. I imagined Regina's admonishment from home. At what seemed to be the halfway mark, I was aware of how ant-like the people were at both the bottom and the top. Was it really only twenty-some minutes? Would they finish on top and come down long before me?

The scarp portion of the mountain did come to an end, and then there was a long walk over rough terrain. My face felt fever-warm, and I was puffing, while hoping to calm down by the time I reached the restaurant area where everyone was to meet. Inside I saw my reflection in a mirror and realized my face was beet red. It took until the group returned before I was breathing naturally, but I was told by several people how red I looked. It had taken me forty-five minutes for the descent. But I made it.

Deja View

There is the almost-senseless panic of being lost in a foreign, exotic, crowded place. I was in Nepal, in Kathmandu. About a mile from my hotel was a colorful, appealing, bazaar-like marketplace with all the enticements I always find irresistible: foods and clothing and oriental objects of art, smells and sounds and sights that mesmerized me, like the young thief of Baghdad come to town.

I had already bought so many treasures to bring home that I needed an additional piece of baggage. Earlier, while with fragments of the group who had chosen to go shopping, I had come upon a merchant who had the perfect bag. It was woven of many brightly colored, shiny threads, and it was special of itself. About two feet long, duffle baggish, with two woven handles, it would serve as a choice carrying bag for Regina upon return. I had happily purchased it and gone back to the hotel with the others. After filling it with excess clothing to make room for purchases in my regular bag, I attempted to zip it closed and discovered the zipper would not work. Hadn't I tried it in the shop? Hadn't it worked then?

I made my way back to the entrance of the marketplace and proceeded in the direction of the shop. What had seemed to be clear in my mind ran together somehow. Did I take a wrong turn? Where are my landmarks? I have a superb sense of direction; where is it? I must have taken a turn too soon or too late. Everything began to look alike. I remember a particular fruit stand at which I had gone to the right; where is that stand?

I retraced my steps. Maybe I need to go back to the beginning and start over. Is this the way now? I tried three or four times. I know I came this way. What's wrong with me? I never forget. Now?

I spent about half an hour trying to locate the merchant. Two schoolboys in their early teens sensed my distress and, in spite of a large language barrier, I felt I had conveyed to them my plight, and they began leading me I know not where. After being led into a courtyard which obviously was not the right place, I begged off. They insisted I follow them up a flight of stairs. I said no, but they persisted, with pleasant smiles on their faces. When, after another "no" from me, they continued to try to get me to follow them, I shook my head, opened the top of my shirt and pointed to the scar from my heart by-pass, indicating that I could not take a flight of stairs. They immediately lost their smiles and backed off. I left the courtyard and felt spared.

I really have no idea whether they were being helpful or whether I was going to be mugged. I prefer to think the former, of course, but I could not take the chance. Too many movies, too many books. Outside the courtyard I felt better, but I still had not found my route.

Almost resigned to chucking the idea, I did spot a familiar sign on a second floor window, and I continued and eventually made my way to the shop.

After showing the non-working zipper to the merchant, he agreed to fix it and asked me to follow him upstairs to where it could be done. Again my imagination began to do me in. Why upstairs? Am I to follow, never to be seen again? But follow I did, and the materials for repair were there, indeed. The zipper was hand-stitched into place, and the bag was presented to me with a smile. He refused extra payment, but I tipped him and left. No one would understand the extreme sense of relief. Actually, no one would understand the panic that brought the need for the relief. It had been a little hairy. Gotta cut out those mysteries.

I strongly believe in extravagance, but I think there is no place for waste.

9

MY UNDERWEAR IS ALL OVER THE WORLD

Living out of a suitcase for so much of the year makes one hone and reshape personal travel habits. My suitcase is the type that serves me best. It is a softside square, with an extendable handle, wheels on what would normally be called the short side, so that tipping over does not happen. I do not follow my own suggestion about traveling with a minimum of clothes. For the typical two-week trip, I pack half a dozen pairs of pants, so that each pair is worn, basically, twice. That's not quite accurate, since a couple of pairs are reserved just for evening wear. I take a good pair of sneakers and two pairs of broken-in walking shoes. I have a separate pair of shoes for the evening. For each day I have a different shirt, with or without a collar, and I have a half-dozen shirts just for the evening. I take no dresswear. I wear white tube socks during most days. I have a pair of undershorts in my belly bag while flying, just in case of a delay, and I have a pair for every day of the trip, plus a couple of extras, just as insurance.

I do not do laundry.

I am as practical as I can be, and I don't want any trip to cost me any more money than necessary; I'm out to make it, not spend it (except for irresistible purchases). But I won't spend my evenings scrubbing my socks and shorts. Therefore, I travel with several plastic bags whose purpose is to house the socks and shorts that will be tied in there and deposited in the garbage upon departure from each hotel. So my underwear is, literally, all over the world, accompanied by my socks. Yes, I do have fears of being notified by the international sanitation department of some far-off place that I am to return to claim it. However, garbage is garbage, and if I am entitled to discard other unwanted material, such as newspapers, what is wrong with my disposing of properly-wrapped underwear? It's just that when I think of how much I have left in so many parts of the world, it seems a little staggering.

I buy those three-packs of Hanes cottons, and the six-packs of socks, knowing that they will have a one-way trip. Considering the cost, it's a small price to pay for the convenience of tossing it all. And obviously I never have old underwear.

I will add that there have been times when I have given used shirts and once-worn socks to a guide to give to anyone who might need them. At the end of a trip in St. Petersburg I had asked our guide if that would be insulting. Could it be given to someone? She readily let me know there was nothing negative about it, and upon departure I gave her a package. As it is usual and acceptable to bring candies and gum and ball-point pens for children in many countries, I felt comfortable to help an adult somewhere with clothing.

Disposing of underwear, socks and, sometimes, other clothing serves another purpose, allowing room for purchases, which, in my own case, is often a problem. I do pack an expandable bag in my regular suitcase because I am in the habit of buying so much. Every extra bit of space helps. When I'm visited at home, people always remark at the amount of "things" that fill my house, always followed by the question, "How did you get it all home?"

I've trained myself to be a hardy traveler. I do not think everything just came naturally or is a matter of constitution. Just as jet lag can be controlled with determination, so, I think, can things like bathroom habits. It is necessary to think ahead in terms of visits to the necessary room; that goes without saying. So one gears oneself as one goes along. In hot climates I am as thirsty as the next person, but I am also aware that the more water one drinks on the bus, the more need there is for a pit stop. A sip instead of a lot is a trained factor that pays off.

In addition, although I almost never take any antibiotics or antihistamines or aspirin or cold medications, I have learned to carry them because someone else always needs them and doesn't have them. Someone always needs a bandaid or a paper clip or a rubber band or an extra luggage lock. The only thing that's always needed but never asked for is a needle and thread. Women always seem to have a needle and thread.

Immodium and Lomotol and similar products are always carried by the people who do not require them. Others and I are always supplying that. I have lost track of the number of packages I have traveled with, never used, and never brought back. However, there never seem to be shortages of hard candies, which I do recommend for long rides on buses.

Once I even supplied an Ace knee brace. I might add that people who take these things never offer to replace them.

Though I will not get into the indelicacies here, I give people suggestions ahead of time on what to do in cases of diarrhea or constipation. I am no doctor and do not want to be criticized for practicing medicine without a license, but on a trip I am depended on for answers to a great variety of questions, without the luxury of a professional to take over. If someone gets sick, I must give the benefit of experience. I don't practice surgery, but folk medicine and home practices do have their place in a crisis. Nausea and fainting are occurrences that one must deal with on the spot. If someone has diarrhea, and I suggest eating rice and bananas, am I really putting them into jeopardy? It always seems to work.

I am not one of those people who take hotel toiletries. I travel with travel-size tooth paste and shampoo. Since shampoo is always provided in the hotels, mine really never gets used, but I have no desire for the little plastic bottles provided. I am not a towel collector. Why take up so much space in the suitcase anyway? I had a cousin who made a practice of taking hotel stationery. Pathetic. And it was from such ordinary hotels. Take it from the Ritz if you're going to take it. And even there, what would I be doing?–impressing someone that I was there? Wouldn't telling them do that?

However, I will admit to having used an occasional hotel plastic laundry bag to garbage my underwear.

Often I find a welcome basket of fruit in my hotel room, compliments of the management as a tour leader. I wish they would leave cheese and crackers instead. I don't do well with fruit on a trip. The three or four times cheese and crackers were left, I made a special effort to express my appreciation. I always express my thanks anyway, but something other than fruit should have something other than the regular thanks.

I do travel with packets of instant hot chocolate for breakfast use in countries where the coffee is too bitter. In that case I ask for a cup of hot water. Other than that, I do not travel with food of any kind except hard candies. If I want biscuits or the like, they are available anywhere. Why bother with the extra stuff in luggage?

I also resist taking food from breakfast to serve as lunch, a practice that does bother me, especially in view of certain people who do it. There are many ways to save money on a trip. That one is just too niggardly for me. I try not to see it when it is done by people who otherwise make the perfect traveler. There are always many choices of places to eat, where costs are insignificant.

Sometimes our flight costs are so unbelievably low, the entire trip is little more than the cost of the plane tickets. When such is the case, and there is no frequent flyer credit, it pains me to have to tell people that there just are no flyer miles. I cannot control that. I explain it in advance. It reminds me of the woman who says she cannot fly unless she has an aisle seat and then one finds her sound asleep for the entire trip in an inside seat. I do the best I can. But the best laid plans of mice and men . . .

I travel with a couple of books because I do not sleep on a plane. I don't like paperbacks, so hardcover books are my one concession to extra weight and space for an otherwise carefully packed person. I never have all my alone time for reading, though. Each evening, as well as some flying time, is spent reviewing itineraries and plans in order to assure coverage of any loose ends for the following days. I practically memorize each next day's printed plans. I remind myself of wake-up calls, tipping procedures, food requests and a plethora of individual requests that mount each day as people expect more and more.

About a week before each trip, my suitcase is placed on the bed of a spare bedroom. Some staples are already in it: folding umbrella, toiletries, the medicines for everyone else, my Camposino hat, sunshield, handkerchiefs, the packages of undershorts and socks, a rain poncho and the like. As the days close in, I add my wardrobe, shoes around the bottom edges, shaver and extra glasses in the center, to be cushioned by the clothing. If I know there will be one-night stops to begin with, I place sets of outfits toward the top, so as not to have to rifle through everything to get a complete outfit. I do not hang clothes up on one-night hotels stays, but I do for two and more nights, partly to prevent wrinkles, partly to air everything.

Regina has her own packing methods, as well, separating many outfits in plastic bags, a habit I've increased, myself. As I wear things, I turn the worn items inside out and place them in the plastic bags, keeping like items together and having them become the bottommost of the packed items, so that as I proceed from destination to destination there is less and less to unpack. As a woman, Regina, of course, travels with many more toiletries, all of which have cleverly designed, inexpensive, vinyl, zippered cases. She also travels with a convertible, collapsible iron, making my grooooming superior when she is with me. When she is not–and I don't iron–I try harder to pack in wrinkle-proof style.

When I buy excessively–and that last word is almost a joke–I use my expandable bag, which then becomes, mostly, the recipient of worn clothing, allowing more space in my regular bag for the purchases, since the regular is sturdier. Between the two of us, Regina and me, we have managed to bring back a few oversized, fragile, impossible treasures such as a tall, brass, Turkish brazier which, fortunately, comes apart in vitally helpful proportions, and a wooden Egyptian chair in the shape of a swan, inlaid with ivory. From Morocco I brought home a great, gaudy mirror that is almost the size of my luggage. It did not break. I even suppose this is the time to re-mention that my house looks like the United Nations gift shop. I have brought back chunks of the world. Bazaars and souks attract me like the smells from a bakery. Even at home, antiques shows and flea markets send out magnetic hooks to me. My middle name is Eclectic.

The family always gathers in anticipation when I open my luggage after a trip, and I am the most excited of us all. Unwrapping my treasures gives me the thrill of a kid in a department store at Christmas time. After years of doing this, each family member manages to stifle some gasping at an occasional bizarre choice, since exotic, heavily carved, grotesque, even weird, choices find a home with me. I wait for the opening words from a first-time visitor. They are usually, "Hey, this is . . . (long pause) . . . interesting." The words come out at the same speed, with the same pause, and the same bail-out,–"interesting." The house is a very decorated place, with very little space on the wall not covered by something unique. I will say I would bet the average person does not have visitors walking around as much as we do. Something always catches the eye, and many, many times I've heard the words, "This is just like a museum!" I take it as a compliment. And I keep shifting things around. Regina tells friends that she never knows what to expect when she comes home: a toilet in the living room, artwork on the ceiling, furniture switched. Hey. It's not boring.

Regina collects penguins and figure-bells. There are hundreds of each all over the house. From one trip alone to Australia and New Zealand, I brought her over forty penguins. I have even bought a penguin in European rural towns where one would think no one knew what a penguin was. The collection ranges in size from half an inch to three feet tall. My collection of a pair of dolls from each country occupies no more than all of two built-in corner closets. The walls of one bedroom are covered with charming folk paintings from China, done in tempera.

When I take a trip without Regina, I leave her little love notes in unlikely places, such as inside the refrigerator and the inside of the toilet seat cover. I can almost hear, see and feel her joy at finding them. And somehow she manages to get to my suitcase when I'm not there, and on various unpacking times of the trip I find similar love notes and cards from her. Yes, they do bring the desired response. I smile as I write.

One of two times my bag was ever inspected was when I went from India into Nepal and back. It was a regular procedure there for the bags of the leader and any one other person to be opened. The second time was in the airport in St. Petersburg when my bag rang the bell because of the lead in a piece of Orrefors crystal I had bought the previous week in Sweden. ???

My bag did not accompany me, and it was the only missing bag, on a return trip from New Zealand. It was early December and extremely cold in New York. I had packed my winter jacket, figuring on retrieving it upon arrival in JFK, a mistake I will never repeat. When the bag did not come through I approached the claims people and explained that I couldn't go out into the parking area in short sleeves. I asked if I could borrow one of the blankets from the plane. They said no, but they did come up with an Abercrombie and Fitch sweater that just happened to be my size. Again, my bag was delivered to my door the next morning.

More than once the feet of my suitcase have run into trouble. Four different times, the suitcase would come out on the carousel conveyor belt, missing one foot. The bag has two feet and two wheels. I have had to have those feet replaced each time. The airlines are never responsible because posted notices inform you that they have no responsibility for protruding portions of luggage. I finally saved myself the continuation of the problem by having a talented local shoemaker remove the remaining foot and replacing both with one longer double rubber foot. The bag is better than when it was new.

So I have at last got packing down to a science. I never travel with a second bag except for return trips with my previously packed, expandable bag. I do not really carry a carry-on. I have a belly-bag which contains all my vital material such as passport, tickets, money, travelers checks, sun glasses, medication, toothbrush and paste, undershorts, and a currency converter. If, indeed, I do take a carry-on, it is not much bigger than a bowling ball bag or a flight bag. And the most it would contain is a book, a crushable hat, hard candies, an extra shirt and whatever outer jacket I wear to the airport. Sometimes my shaver and camera go into that bag.

So much for packing habits.

10

TOILET TRAINING

I guess toilets figure into my life more than I would think. But now that I'm thinking, I realize how much thought I do give to them.

First of all, I do not like using public toilets. I only like using a toilet at home and in hotel rooms. When I do use a public toilet, I am one of those people who must first wipe the seat and then cover it with a length of toilet paper. I'm glad the days of those small folded sheets have passed; they always seemed to slide into the toilet before I was finished lining the seat. And on trains and planes the upcoming draft was like a suction cup.

I don't like the new, large toilet paper dispensers that are parallel to the wall. They're always too low. It's hard to find where the paper starts, and once you've torn paper from the roll you can't find the beginning of the roll again. Half the time you have to bend halfway over to get at it. Other times, you roll and roll it and still can't find the beginning.

It was much simpler with the old-fashioned types of regular-sized rolls which came out perpendicularly from the wall.

In Europe there are many public toilets in presentable places, such as restaurants, which are not what we have come to call Western-style. The fixture is sometimes the same, but there's no raisable seat. How do you use that? You don't sit on the bare porcelain. If you have to straddle it without contacting it, why make it so wide? The width is to accommodate the seated butt.

Why put the handle where it is intended to be touched by a hand? I wouldn't put my hand on one of those dirty handles. Even if it's high, I use my foot. That is, the sole of my shoe, of course.

And why, in proper places, is there so often no paper?

I remember having to use a toilet on the road once in Turkey. We even stopped there because it was one of the *better* rest stops. It is a common practice throughout the rest of the world to charge a small fee for using a toilet. It always annoyed me, but that's because, I'm sure, I just wasn't used to it. It does make sense, I suppose, and people get accustomed to having coins with them for that purpose.

At this particular toilet, the attendant handed out toilet paper when you paid the small amount (probably two cents). I was handed a strip of blue (*blue?*) toilet paper, four squares long. I resisted the temptation to ask, "What could I possibly do with *this?* I still don't know what anyone would do with toilet paper the length of one tissue. Is there something I should know?

The stalls inside had no doors. There were also no fixtures, just a drain where the toilet would stand, with a small bucket of water against the stall wall. So one had to squat and aim (whoever thinks of aiming?) and then pour the bucket of water on top of the result. Can anyone really think this is a better way?

The first time I realized there could be female attendants in a men's room was at the Folies Bergere. I was very young, and I had gone down the stairs to the men's room. On my way out, a hand extended itself from a closet at the foot of the stairs, palm up. An old woman was on the other end of the hand. A tip was in order.

It still is disconcerting to me when I am standing at a urinal, and a woman mops the floor around me.

In one quality restaurant in Rome, the necessary coed room contained three stalls in a row. The first one had a conventional Western toilet with an abused, chintzy plastic seat, but a seat nevertheless; the second one had a toilet with no seat at all; the third one had just the drain in the center of the floor. Ye pays yer money and ye takes yer cherce. That anyone prefers other than the good old U.S.A. standard brand amazes me.

I also wonder what the fee, however tiny, is for. No lavatory I ever used seemed better for having an attendant. Most are memorable for being dirty, wet or smelly or all three. Rarely is there paper; rarely are there paper towels. Public bathrooms in the rest of the world are decidedly behind us, if you'll pardon that word.

The worst are on trains. Toilet *train*-ing. On a train from Vienna into Crakow, the condition was so bad, I decided against my need. On a twelve-hour ride in Peru, from Puno to Cusco, my need was too great to give up. The bathroom could turn a stomach. The floor was wet as well as littered. The toilet looked like a disease-breeder. The door had no lock and would not stay closed. Everything rattled. The stench could cause an up-chuck. I can't even believe I went.

Airports in small cities of Third World countries are almost equally disgusting. It's when I visit these places that I ask myself if I'm really a traveler. Why don't I take all this in stride? Well, as a matter of fact, I do take it all in stride. That doesn't mean I can't hate that part of it. And hate it I do. Boy, the times I have resisted the urge to use a bathroom. I'm glad my constitution listens to me.

I do travel with a packet of toilet seat covers and a supply of tissues. Obviously there are times and places when and where the covers are pointless, but I am tuned in to the fact that many people ask if someone has tissues. This is one thing I really don't carry for someone *else's* benefit.

And the plane. I don't like to use the plane lavatories, which I, of course, do use. Here it's more the awkwardness that someone is waiting and thinking I'm taking forever. Well, that's my own hangup, for sure, but it's there. It also amazes me that the lavatories aren't attended to. Halfway through a flight, the toilet paper is gone and the room is filthy. I think an attendant should check in there once in a while. I always try to get there before the rush after mealtime. It's amazing: the moment the trays are removed, the entire planeload has to go.

And is there anybody besides myself (aren't I the perfect old traveler, now) who thinks about the person in the seat in front of me? When someone leaves his seat, he pulls for all he's worth on the seat in front of him. I know you need some kind of support with those angles and lack of space, but sometimes I think the person behind me is trying to remove the seat. And when he replaces his tray, it's often with such force, I expect to be shoved forward a seat. And how much rummaging must he do in the netted holder beneath the tray? What has he got in there that requires so much jiggling, pulling and pushing?

The toilet on the bus. Well, I've discussed that a bit already. I have never used it, and I look forward to never using it again. On touring buses, that toilet is generally adjacent to the steps of the rear door. Just the attention would bother this shy soul. In the States, when buses have only the door in the front, the toilet is way in the rear of the bus. Well, the people seated back there have to understand. It seems a little better to me, but maybe that's because it's on the same level with the rest of the bus. On the foreign ones, at the rear door, one has to descend a step or two and then enter. Buses jiggle. As the saying goes, "Will the men please sit, too?"

Men, of course, have an easier, faster time using public toilets. When the stop is only for watering purposes, men don't have to remove anything. Fewer men travel, and they are faster, so lines before men's rooms are shorter. When the visit is for a greater purpose, that's when men realize how much more difficult it is for women. It also makes a dry floor more appreciated. As leader, I'm in the habit, when the last man has gone, of making the men's room a second ladies' room. It's only fair.

The cigarette burns in public bathrooms outnumber burns elsewhere. Aside from the miserable smell and the ugliness of it, I can't help but think, "You put your cigarette down and then put it back onto your lips?" The burns are on every horizontal surface you can find.

So many toilets have too little space around them. When you get inside the door, you have to stand sideways to close the door before you can do anything about your clothing and sit. More often than not there is no hook for any clothing. Where can you put anything?—over the door? Most people wear a belly bag. Switching its position so that the bag itself is in the back is not always a snap. I unhook mine and wear it around my neck. If I have any more than that to contend with, I ask someone ahead of time to hold it. Stalls are not accessories-friendly.

The countless times the toilet is filled to the top when you enter. Yuk. It certainly can't be used. When I think of the uninviting bathrooms I've encountered in various parts of my own country, I immediately recall how much worse are those around the world, where, literally, I avoid going when I really need to, because I cannot face what appears to be a cesspool. Who doesn't spend a lot of time in bathrooms, at home and in hotels? I have finished entire books in bathrooms. Maybe it's to make up for all the times I turned away in public places. I have somewhat staunch sanitation needs. I mean, I fear the Bubonic Plague, the Black Death, syphilis, gonorrhea, the crud, you name it. Maybe one doesn't contract those things from toilets, but that doesn't mean one doesn't think about it.

11

STRAINED BEDFELLOWS

It's a common and natural request. Someone wants to take a tour but has no traveling companion, wants to share a room primarily to save the expense of a single supplement. Yes, the reason is that someone might not want to be alone in a room at night, but mostly it's because the supplement is a good percentage higher than the regular price of a trip, based per person on double occupancy. So prior to almost every trip I am asked if I can match someone with a roommate. My success record is really quite high, but there are exceptions.

Nancy, whom I knew a little, and Katherine, whom I did not know at all. Each was married, each wanted a roommate, each was about fifty.

Nancy said, "The only request I make is that she does not snore."

"Well, Nancy, that's something I couldn't possibly promise. How could I know that?"

Katherine only said, "I just want someone pleasant. I'm easy."

I gave each the other's phone number, and they managed to meet for lunch one day prior to our departure. Nancy was obviously the stronger of the two women. I hoped she wouldn't browbeat Katherine, a sweet, less secure personality.

On the flight over, Nancy repeated to me, "I just hope she doesn't snore."

On the second day of the trip, I asked Katherine how it seemed to be going. "Fine," she answered, "except that I was up all night because Nancy snores so much."

A girl in her late twenties wanted to take a trip but had no companion. A guy about the same age, engaged to be married, wanted the same trip, but his fiancee would not be coming. The two roomed together, and the match was perfect.

Not a single problem.

A bachelor in his forties signed on for a trip as a single. An eighty-two-year-old woman wanted the same trip but did not want the single supplement. The bachelor had the only single. She said she would be perfectly happy to room with the man. At her request, I called him to tell him of her proposal. He cancelled his reservation.

Olga, an outspoken, strong-willed woman asked for a roommate. (I could not know she was not roommate material). Mary, one of the friendliest women I know, agreed to share with her. Only after several days did Mary tell me Olga kept waking her to tell her she breathed too loudly and snored. Mary spent the previous night sleeping in the bathtub. I told her I would kill her if she did that again. "If Olga has the problem, tell *her* to sleep in the goddamn bathtub!"

Olga would tell someone with a cold not to sit near anyone on the bus. I had already asked that anyone with a cold try not to infect anyone else. It's a tacky situation. People with colds have isolated themselves as much as possible. When there was only one empty seat at a long table we were sharing for dinner, and that person with the cold tried to sit there, Olga told her to go and find another table. This table had been reserved for us.

"*You* go and find another table, goddamn it!" I bellowed, not caring who heard or what my job was. "Where do you get off telling people where to sit on the bus and whether they can sit at our table? Maybe the reason the only empty seat was next to you is because nobody wants to sit there! Ever think of anyone else's feelings? Nobody wants anyone's cold, but she's doing everything she can, not to breathe on anyone. You want her to stop breathing altogether?"

But what can you expect when, objecting to the close driving of a native of the country as we were walking, she spat on his windshield in anger?

Helen, a tyrant in her own way, asked for a roommate like one I had arranged for her on a previous trip. "She was a personal friend of mine, and I told you then she was the best," I replied. "But I haven't got another like her for this trip. There's just one elderly lady who would like a roommate, but I know you won't care for her."

"Oh, it'll be okay," Helen responded. "After all, it's just to sleep."

Famous last words. The hotel issued only one key per room, no matter the request for individual keys. The elderly woman got the key first and would not surrender it. If Helen wanted to go to the room, she first had to find her roommate. "Why can't you just leave it at the desk?" she asked, logically.

"Because it has the name of the hotel on it. I always take a walk, and I'm afraid of getting lost."

"In the first place, Bob asked us never to walk alone. This is Third World. In the second place, why can't you, then, just write the hotel name on a piece of paper, for Pete's sake?"

Once, I was certain I had made the match of matches. Two retired teachers. About the same age, and, I assumed, similar dispositions. One had been with me on several trips, the other, though new, seemed most compatible. They met at the airport, not at the orientation, because only one was able to attend the orientation.

For the first couple of days, my calculation seemed correct. Then the undercurrent began to swell. If one of two is strong-willed, the meeker one cowers. So it seemed to be. Ms. Timid told me that Ms. Bold rose early, made lots of noise, rattled around, doing exercises; Ms. Bold complained that Ms. Timid kept her belongings all over the room, and was a druggie and a drinker. Ms. Timid told me quietly; Ms. Bold told me loudly. Ms. Timid said Ms. Bold had no kindness or understanding; Ms. Bold told me Ms. Timid was cracked. Ms. Bold couldn't stand Ms. Timid's whimpering; Ms. Timid couldn't take Ms. Bold's bellowing.

I never knew about Ms. Timid's drugs or drinking. Ms. Bold, new to me, had come across as a take-it-as-it-is, go-with-the-flow type. Well, you never know someone till you share a bathroom, I guess. They sat further and further apart on bus rides, and whoever was near them heard the story. The situation did not improve, and passengers do not want to hear roommates' regrets, so they come to my ears. (Do you remember the old radio program with Mr. Anthony, solving everyone's problems)?

At every orientation, I invited everyone to let me know if they had problems that I could help solve, such as health concerns, constipation or the trots, language barriers, tipping procedures, VAT (value-added tax), wherein there is a return of the amount of tax paid on certain purchases in certain countries upon exiting, and most people get confused. I offered every kind of help. But I never mentioned relationships, except to repeat that friendships made on trips enhance the trips. (Social counsellor did not come up).

Since most people get along extremely well most of the time on most of the trips, the difficult times stand out. I have worked very hard at mediating, but sometimes I want to put my head in the sand. When roommate pairing has been my doing, I feel a great responsibility, of course. Mis-matching is rare, but when it happens, oh, boy. I never even liked blind dates.

Somewhere, some time ago, I read that there is no bore like a travel bore . . . No one is the least bit interested in your trip to Hong Kong.

Whoever said that, please accept my appreciation and my blessings. You have said it all.

Well, Maybe not all . . .

It's a two-week trip. On the second day a woman sees another woman on the bus and says, "I know I could never like her. She's not my type." On the fourth day she finds herself seated next to the woman for breakfast, at the end of which she says, "She's not so bad, after all. Maybe I had her pegged wrong." On the sixth day she says, "I think we'll become fast friends after this." On the eighth day she says, "You know, she's beginning to annoy me now. Maybe I should have heeded my first impression." On the tenth day she says, "Uch, I can't stand her." On the twelfth day she says, "Oh, she's really not so bad." On the last day she says, "Next time, why don't we share a room?"

12

CLIENTELE/CLIENT HELL

No one likes to be pigeon-holed, stereotyped, caricatured. I don't want to do that to people. However, one cannot be in this business very long without realizing in magnification how stereotypical people do become. There is a point at which, in describing people, you almost want to say, "He's a 'D', she's a 'K.'" It would save time in talking about them, when, indeed, you must talk about them, and, indeed, you must talk about them.

The average person wants to think he's not average, but I almost see a set of cubby holes, like the ones behind the registration desks in hotels; you have a number, and that's where the clerk reaches. You are 206 or 717 or 1210.

I try never to talk about travels unless I'm asked. And even then I try not to go on too long. Let the people guide you in that case. Let them let you know how much you should go on. Travelers go on too much. No one talks about anything as much as travelers talk about travel. It bores those who've been and alienates those who haven't.

Unfortunately for you, I will repeat this.

TYPES

JUDY JUDY JUDY

I had the misfortune of being seated next to her on the side of a plane that had just two seats in each row. There was not a third party to diffuse the talk. The opening was about her extensive travel, the number one stereotypical repeat. She spent a cruel amount of time telling me about her three sons, one a doctor, one a lawyer, one an engineer. Of course. Maybe she didn't have a fourth because he'd have had to be an Indian chief. They had gone to the best colleges and were tops in their classes. She then progressed to telling me that she loved to do the puzzles in the Sunday *Times*; it was her favorite thing. She was a docent in a small museum/gallery. She loved art and art history. She was taking this trip to expand her horizons in that area. I thought of that often, during the trip, when she paid very little attention to the guide who expounded with the information she should have relished. She also mentioned, as we went from ruin to ruin, that it's all just a bunch of stones. This was followed by a giggle and the pronouncement that that's her sense of humor, something I never found.

Tipping on trips is minimal, and it is a subject I explain thoroughly ahead of time, at the orientation a month prior to the trip. Two dollars a day for an outstanding guide was something she managed to balk at and/or avoid. Though she spoke at length about going here and there and buying this and that, the only time I saw her spend anything, it was for a small bag of nuts. Besides being one who does all of the above ad nauseum, her chatter is endless. She is certainly bright, but I don't understand how someone as bright as she, fails to hear some of what she says and fails to think at some point that she talks but does not listen. The need to impress is so dominant it suppresses the ability to hear anything anyone else says. Others on the trip have her "credentials." Others have traveled, have educated, prosperous children, do the *Times* crossword, read, visit museums, articulate without boasting. Why do they manage not to have to etch all this into every person they talk to? Why can Judy not grasp what is happening?–that the others kindly wait out her rambling without ever having to ask if they can have a turn at showing off?

Judy is also the one who, during the question/answer period following a library lecture, will raise her hand not to ask a real question of the speaker, but to waste everyone's time in letting them know where she's been.

Judy has many clones, and every trip has one (or more), and only the Judies don't understand that they're Judies and everyone has their number.

It is difficult for me to listen to one-time two-week visitors who speak with authority about a country.

ALLEGRA AND ARIADNE

I first met Allegra on a day trip of the Hudson Valley. I used to do many of those trips. We would visit a historical mansion in the morning, then stop for lunch and visit two more mansions in the afternoon. The group was always similar, mostly women traveling in pairs. Allegra traveled alone and looked a little different from the others, plainer and more simply attired–a plain cotton dress and sneakers–and she wore her hair combed simply back. She was tiny and quiet, and showed no expression. Often she slept while the bus was in motion, but once we arrived at a site, she was most animated and attentive.

It was probably on the third trip that she was first accompanied by her daughter Ariadne. Ariadne was in her thirties and much taller than her mother. She walked with some difficulty, using her toes but not her heels, her feet pointing in and her gait something of a sway. She was an elementary school teacher with a mind much more inquisitive than any of her students could have. With Ariadne, Allegra was more animated.

Rarely did anything prevent Ariadne from a point of interest. On a weekend trip to Cape May, we stopped at the bird sanctuary on our way home. The lighthouse there is an optional visit which most people avoid, either because they relax at that part of the trip and just do the walks around the area, looking for birds, or because it's too difficult a haul up those many winding stairs. Ariadne certainly did it. She puffed, but she did it.

When we returned from that trip to the spot where the bus had picked up everyone, Allegra and Ariadne found themselves without a ride home. Regina and I offered to take them home. It was only a short drive. As soon as we arrived, Allegra insisted we take a seat on their lawn, and she disappeared into the house, while we talked with Ariadne. Moments later, Allegra appeared with a tray full of unusual Greek food concoctions, and she happily served them with a smile that has come to be known to me as precious, and the two of them charmed the two of us.

Some time after that I led a group to Turkey. It was in February, and there was still a good deal of snow on the mountains in Cappadocia. It takes a bit of maneuvering to wend through the hills and caves of Cappadocia when the ground is clear and dry. But here and now snow covered our paths in many instances. Allegra climbed over rocks that were tall for a taller person than she, and she got herself through winding and tricky caves. Ariadne took more time, but missed nothing. Her biggest handicap is steps with no railing, and the good people around her always lent her a hand, which she took when necessary.

When it was time to descend, Ariadne simply sat down on her coat and slid her way down the mountainside. She did this repeatedly wherever necessary. Never a complaint from either.

Mother and daughter had packing down to their own science. They correctly traveled with a minimum of clothing and boarded the plane with two small, though expandable, bags. I learned early on that they shop. I mean "shop." Ariadne, for example, has a thing for rugs. Turkey is a rug place. Ariadne bought rugs. I kept asking her how she was going to get them home; was she sending them? Of course not. Well, when finally we did leave, those two small bags had swollen larger than body bags. I do think they outweighed me by a ton, but they made it home, and that's how the two of them travel.

Their experience outdoes that of most people who've traveled with me. They have done the most unusual forms of traveling. Once they drove on a road in the southwestern U.S. because they'd learned that it led to Georgia O'Keeffe's house. They had car trouble and came upon a roadblock, but they managed to find a ranger who got them out. They've gone to countries most people don't think about. Their home is a treasure trove of unusual things they've brought back, and their display of it is unique. Sports galore, their buying is special.

I must say, as I've said to her, Ariadne's buying makes me crazy because we're always waiting for her. It seems I spend a great deal of time counting heads, then going back to the last place where things were being sold, and seeing Ariadne's blushing, guilty, sweet smile and hearing, "I'm coming, I'm coming." There is always someone who is late. Once is okay, twice not too bad, but when it gets to three times for the same person, the group justifiably gets annoyed. It's my job to prevent that. Ariadne is the only one about whom I squirmed. If anybody else was consistently late, I accepted the group's annoyance and agreed with it and got starchy with the perpetrator, but with Ariadne it was always more difficult for me. Yet, what could I do? There were times when I had to pressure her. Since we sometimes had to wait because she was slower than the group, it wasn't fair of her to add to the waits. It was sticky. But she understood. She didn't always move, but she understood.

I was arranging for a trip to Greece and the Greek Islands. They signed up. I asked Allegra why she was coming on this trip. She came from Greece, went there regularly, and, to top it off, had just come back from a six-week stay there. I asked her why she was coming on this trip after all that. With her priceless, almost impish smile, she said, in her accent, "I haven't been there with *you*."

While climbing up the steep steps of Delphi, I noticed her stopping for a moment, more than once, to catch her breath, which wasn't coming easily. "Why are you doing this?" I asked.

"I want to," she said simply, with that smile.

"But maybe it's too much," I said.

"So what's going to happen?" she said. "I'm going to die?" She smiled.

"Don't you do that here!" I said.

"Can you think of a better place?" she smiled.

Allegra has told other people that she's very sad that I've given up leading groups. She wants to continue traveling, but she only wants to go with me. I really love her and would want to continue just to make her happy.

We see the two women regularly. At their home they serve ten times as much as is necessary and force you to take home enough for three days. And if they visit you, they bring so many things that you have to put your hands to your head. What a rare pair of gems.

One month after the writing of this book, Ariadne called to say that her mother had had a heart attack and passed away. All through the church service and the funeral, I kept hearing her words, "Bob, I don't want to travel without you."

Allegra, Bob doesn't want to travel without you, either. The memory of you will be forever, you wonderful, fabulous lady. There's no one like you. Rest in peace.

EVERY LITTLE BREEZE SEEMS TO TWITTER

It would never occur to Louise that she is infuriating. I know in her mind she is sweet and well-intentioned, always making suggestions that would have to enhance my life, always asking for something that is not included. She, too, does her homework before each trip, and a week before departure she calls me to say something like . . . "We're going to be only about forty miles from—could we stop there?" Or, "While we're in—wouldn't it be nice to have dinner with a family from there?" Or, "Since the opera is in season, could you work something out whereby we might sit in on a rehearsal?"

Louise is a vegetarian. There are often three or four vegetarians in our group. It almost never presents a problem. They know to call in to the airlines to arrange for a vegetarian meal on the plane. Vegetarians are always served before the others. Since breakfasts and dinners are always included on my trips, lunches can be anything the vegetarians choose. Breakfasts are almost exclusively vegetarian anyway. That leaves dinner. I try to have an option of fish because it's a variation in the first place and because it's more variety for the vegetarians in the group. There is never a problem in getting vegetarian meals. Even then, those meals are generally served before the regular ones. Once, just once, when fish was being prepared specially, in a very crowded dining room, the regular dinners were served first. Louise sat glaring at me and asked why everyone had been served and she had to wait. All those countless early times had vanished from her memory.

When it has happened that some stray non-vegetarian item appeared on her plate, Louise automatically placed it onto mine (I tried not to sit with her, and though I was largely successful, there were times when it was unavoidable, plus: she generally asked to sit with me). I always told her I didn't want it, and her answer was always, "But I know you like it." It happened too often, and I've explained that I get turned off when someone does that to me, so when she did it, I stopped eating altogether. When she asked why, and I explained that I cannot eat when someone puts his food onto my plate (just call it a "thing"), it would not register, and at a subsequent meal it would happen again. Finally, I had to state firmly, "Louise, I've told you that I can't eat when someone dumps his plate onto mine! Would you please stop doing it!" She made the face of a sorrowful child and said, "I meant well."

I've already stated that I buy many things on a trip and that my home looks like the United Nations Gift Shop. Since Louise, like the others, attends the orientations at my home, she would tell me, in a shop, that I should have this or that. I smile and say nothing, and she persists. She buys little other than postcards and tiny, inexpensive items, but she picks out lavish things for me to buy. I have definite taste, and I enjoy the fact that we all like something different. I get pleasure from someone's enjoyment and excitement; I enjoy it when someone tells me what excites them, even if, as often happens, it's too expensive to purchase. Being pressured by someone, though, to buy something because that person feels it belongs in my house, is a step too far. I also don't really want that person to stay with me while I'm browsing. I shop and buy conscientiously; I don't want the distraction. It seems that on every trip there is one large, impractical, expensive item that I have to have. I more than sense people's excitement in seeing whether I do, indeed, buy it. Louise fastens herself to me at those times.

I find that Louise does have exquisite taste. (How often the word "exquisite" is followed by the word "taste"). The things she admires are fine and elegant. So are the things I like, but I am also often attracted to the gaudy and grotesque. I only know that many things catch my eye, and it wouldn't bother me at all to ask another's opinion, but when someone suggests strongly, and practically forces me to become interested in something, I have a problem.

A couple of times I noticed that when Louise made a purchase, she said to the salesman, "I am usually presented with some small gift when I buy something." The first time I heard her say that, I gulped. The second time, I moved away. She makes it work, though.

Another habit Louise has is to become over-friendly with the guide, to the point of walking with her arm around that guide if it happens to be a female and very close when a male. When we are walking as a group to a particular site the guide is about to explain, that habit is annoying because the guide has been hooked into Louise's attention, and the group must wait for their conversation to end. Most guides are aware of this and able to handle it, but sometimes there's a new, young, enthusiastic guide who's afraid to be rude, so I must say, "Louise, we're all waiting . . ."

She asks many personal questions of the guide, unrelated to the tour, and then relates to the group what she's learned, because now she has a personal relationship. Meanwhile, the guide is more or less forced to walk with Louise from site to site.

Louise gets cosily friendly with various people on the trips, but she never really cares for anyone and never sees them afterwards. She uses many "dears" in her conversations, and it seems that she is forming many friendships, but no one cares for her, and everything ends when the trips ends. When she talks to me about her new acquaintances, she makes flattering, kind remarks, most of which change toward the end of the trip, all of which lead nowhere, and none of which seem to be sincere.

To me, as well, she says glittering things. In my presence she flatters me constantly to others at a table. Her compliments are flowery and quite beautiful, actually, but after a number of years I know that it's all veneer and gloss. And others, possibly more astute than I, seem to get her number after a much shorter period of time. She requires recognition and attention. When ordering in a restaurant or dining room, she is one of those people whose need for special service is a fulfillment of the need for attention: this on the side, this done in this way, this served only after this, with a twist of this, is it fresh (!), my compliments to the chef, and all that other crap . . .

Her voice is faint, and she makes no effort to raise it if you struggle to hear her. You are required to move closer and to ask her to repeat, at which time she furrows her brow a bit as if to express difficulty in speaking any louder. There have been a few times, however, when she wanted something in a hurry, and volume somehow was available.

Louise is quite tall, and her carriage is good, and she dresses in flattering outfits which are correct for her, but when she appears on the scene, it is obvious that her poise/pause is for acknowledged admiration. Each night, though the atmosphere is always casual, and the group assumes that casualness, Louise becomes Joan Crawford until she eats and forgets.

There are evenings, of course, when we have entertainment. It could be a belly dancer in Turkey or Morocco, a night club act in Paris or Rome or one of those spectacular shows in Beijing. Whatever it is, we have a group reservation, and not once has Louise failed to have the seat closest to the performers, whether it's on a stage or a dance floor. I've tried to discover how she does it. She's been on many trips with me. I have never learned her secret. Is there such a thing as a pawky pusher?–a subtle slitherer? When it happens on trip after trip, others are aware, too, and they don't seem to discover her secret. I do hear a lot of "How the hell does she always do it?"

During a trip to China, she asked me to arrange to get to see craftsmen at work. We had come to Beijing from Shanghai. Visits to cloissonne factories and silk shops and carpet shops and Friendship stores were already built into the trip. She insisted we make a special "optional" trip to "see the real thing". Well, optional, of course, always means extra costs. I explained that *even* in the Third World guides know where to take tourists and receive kickbacks on purchases. She was certain that there were places, though, where we would see the *real* thing; couldn't we go there?

"Louise," I said, "there are so many places we will be visiting. I honestly don't know the legitimacy of a place I haven't been to."

"Well," she replied, "just tell him what we want."

Side trips are called side trips because that's what they are. They're on the side, and you reach into your side pocket to get the extra money they will cost. If you want to go by bus, the guide will come up with a price the bus will cost for this extra jaunt. You have to find out how many people are interested, and they all chip in. Louise's persuasiveness induced a large enough number of people to warrant getting the bus. I had to trust the guide, whom I had not known, and we would have an afternoon of "specified shopping."

After two stops, it was obvious that we were taken to places where we could be "taken". There was the typical flourishing sales pitch with the serving of tea. The goods were shown or modeled or dangled, and the prices were painful. I never disguised my thoughts—I, who am capable, through training, of a perfect poker face. In this situation I felt little responsibility beyond giving my opinion. Normally, if I feel there is undue sales pressure or anything less than above-board, I move right in and stop the show. Once, in Egypt, I felt salesmen applying pressure to naive travelers in my group, and I immediately went to the proprietor and said, "These men do not know I am the group leader. If they don't back off, I will take everyone out right now." And my groups do accept my judgment. Quite often they ask for my opinion before a purchase. When I know, I know. And since I am looked to for guidance, I must be certain, careful, caring and honest. When he conveyed his message to his salesmen, they all looked at me, and the atmosphere changed. They humbled, and kept looking for my approval.

In this situation, which I did not create, I did not interfere; I only showed my disdain. It is also customary for the guide to let the salespeople know I'm the tour leader. (In many instances they offer me a discount or a gift for allowing the group to come there). It had not been mentioned that I was the leader. In short time, the group got the message and understood my position. Even Louise, this time, realized, although there never would have been an acknowledgement from her.

It turned out to be a waste of time and money, but a good lesson came of it, and it was better for me as well because it was in the earlier stages of my leading, and those who took subsequent trips with me have said, "If Bob says 'stay away', then stay away." I hadn't considered the vote-of-confidence factor it would give me, but Louise unknowingly gave me that. When people travel with you over and over, their reliance and trust are important—to them and to the people they recommend.

I guess it's a kind of flirting that Louise engages in. When we enter, say, a carpeting concern, she shows great interest to the man who runs the show. He, of course, feels he has someone who is an important buyer. They talk at length about carpets that cost thousands of dollars. I know that Louise is never going to buy even a doily, but we must wait through this game she, for some reason, insists on playing. If you multiply this charade times the number of commercial places you visit, it is easy to lose patience because, in the first place, there are people who prefer not to visit shops at all, and the ones who want to visit do not want to waste time. And that's what Louise does: she wastes time. There are more important things to do than to pretend, for whatever reason, that you're going to buy. It's often difficult to wait for the serious shoppers. Allotting the fair share of time at sites and shopping is one of the most irking tasks of a tour leader. What is too much for some people is not enough for others. Louise also shows impatience when her own interest is limited, disregarding the interest of others. Most frustrating.

Her "dear"'s run thin as the trip winds down, and it is generally at that time that she tells me we haven't sat together "for a long time" at dinnertime. I think she feels the growing alienation she has caused, though I don't think she would ever admit it. But others in the group, by that time, have tried to avoid her.

She is annoying on the plane. As with most groups, we fly economy class. Louise always goes into the business section to use the lavatory. If she were a passenger in business class, she would be the first one to berate someone who does what she does, but she finds excuses for herself.

During one three-country/three-city trip, she complained that the hotel in the first city was not centrally located; in the second city the hotel had rooms of varying sizes, and there were others larger than hers; in the third city, the centrally located hotel was too noisy because of its central location.

There are people who ask me to tell them if she is signing up for a particular trip, because they would prefer not to go if she does. It would shock her to learn who they are; they are the very people she feels like her the most—just as there are times when people ask if we could leave her behind at a particularly crowded spot. It has happened so often. How well I remember one woman on that China trip, who said, while we were cruising on the river, "If she doesn't knock it off, I'm going to deep-six her!"

It would bother Louise terribly to learn this about herself, but, then, I think she has the ability to disbelieve it even if an entire group were to say it. She has imagined herself an ideal person, and there would be no possibility of altering that in her mind. She has created this image that she's certain the world sees. I somewhat envy that. What a way to get out of seeing what's really in the mirror.

SHE DOES HAVE GRACE

She looked like the grandmother of the world. EVERYGRAND MOTHER! She had once-blond hair, pulled back into a bun and braided across the top. She was sweet-faced and plump. She wore thick glasses and a hearing-aid, and she walked with a cane. I envisioned her in an apron, with cookies in her pocket for her grandchildren, with an apple pie cooling on the window sill. She, too, came to me via a Hudson Valley day trip. On the way home from one trip, the subject of future trips always came up; I never had to bring it up, because someone always did. After mentioning a coming trip to the Holy Land, Grace asked me upon arrival home whether I would consider taking her along. It was such an awkward, humble, self-effacing question. Why would I not?

In her soft Georgian drawl Grace told me that she'd been widowed the previous year; her husband had never wanted to travel. It was something she had always wanted to do but was unable to because of his refusal. Now, at seventy-eight, she wanted to see as much of the world as she could, but was afraid her vision and hearing difficulties, as well as her need of a cane, when put together with her age, might make her undesirable in a group, and she felt unable to go independently. She was quick to say she wouldn't allow anyone to help her with her baggage, that she traveled light anyway, and that if there were sites for which she might be too slow, she would wait for everyone at the starting point, rather than hold anyone up. Since this was Israel, she would visit everything she could, and if there were hills, she'd catch up with the group or remain at the point of arrival, even if the heat was intense.

I probably began to love her at that point. It was the day we'd met, and she'd decided on the basis of that one-day trip that she could entrust herself to me on her first foreign venture. I listened to that sweet Southern sound, realized this was a totally good person who wanted to spend her twilight years catching up, and I was going to take care of her.

Though only a deposit was required for registration, Grace submitted the entire payment. At Kennedy Airport, she appeared with what seemed to be an overnight satchel, and that represented her total luggage. She sat quietly on the plane, and, most of the times I checked on her, she slept. I soon became aware of the absence of her peripheral vision; one had to get pretty much in front of her to be noticed, and then one saw how extremely thick her lenses were. And once in a while, when you began to speak to her, she would touch her hearing aid briefly, as if to set it. She made no unnecessary conversation but was sweetly pleasant when talked to. She did not encourage conversation, but there was no absence of warmth because of that.

Whenever she entered a dining room, she would pause to get her bearings and focus. Almost timidly, she would ask if it was all right to join whatever table she approached. She ate heartily and whatever there was, never asking for anything. She was always early for the bus, to avoid the possibility of having anyone wait for her. She graciously followed the "rule" that we alternate our seating so that everyone would have a chance to sit in various sections of the bus; this she did in spite of the fact that it would have been much easier for her always to sit near the door. It bothered her to have to be helped down from the bus. Many people accept the same help, but without much thought. And I learned early that she tipped the driver extra at the end of the trip just because he offered his hand.

Grace never took photographs because she was unable to, but I saw that she bought postcards to take their place. She never shopped, but never showed impatience while others did. She did mention once that she was at the time of her life where she was more interested in disposing of things than collecting more. (Will I ever realize that point)?

When there was a special evening, such as going from the hotel to entertainment or dinner elsewhere, she never said it's too late or too much or too far. She merely added earrings and beads and joined the crowd. The others always happily took turns in walking with her, helping her on stairs and looking for her. Still not much talk, but she won everyone's hearts. Her determination, spirit and goodness won over everyone, though it was not mentioned at any time by her. Whenever it was time to leave a site, one knew that everyone silently looked to make sure Grace was there, which she always was. Often I feared the pace might be too much, but she kept up, pausing every now and then to wipe her brow with her handkerchief. She puffed when she caught up with everyone, but catch up she did. I walked with her whenever I was not required to be in the lead. Regularly I had the thought that her grandchildren must think she's the most precious person in the world; I hoped that was so.

I looked for her every few minutes while we walked and visited sites, to be sure she was all right. There were times when I really wondered whether she was hearing everything there was to hear, seeing all there was to see. The bus portions of the trips were her catching-up time. She renewed her strength by getting ample rest on the ride, while most people talked. I silently smiled when I heard different people engage her in conversation, however brief, and when they invited her to sit with them at mealtime, and mostly when they helped her on stairs and in difficult areas.

To know she was having a good time gave me great pleasure.

Grace was not one you would want to seek to engage in conversation, because she didn't actually promote it. There was no small talk. She was essentially quiet and felt no need for unnecessary conversation. Inasmuch as most people, including myself, overtalk on trips, she was a refreshment. If it seemed awkward to say little, one had to realize it was not awkward for *her*, so there was no need to go on. There was something restful about that.

When the Holy Land trip was over, we flew from Tel Aviv to Paris, with a short layover before continuing to the U.S. While waiting in the airport for our connecting flight, Grace approached me and quietly said, "Bob, I've been meaning to give this to you," and she handed me an envelope. Naively, I couldn't imagine what it was. It was, of course, a tip. I don't know how much there was in there; I just saw that it was money and handed it right back to her.

"Grace, you don't have to tip me," I said.

"But I want to make sure you'll take me on future trips," she answered.

"Grace," I said, "I don't take tips. But of course I would take you. On any trip you wanted. But you don't have to tip me."

"But I want to," she replied. And she praised the trip and my attention.

I thanked her for even the gesture, and her presence on all future trips only enhanced them for me. Oddly, the trips she subsequently took were the most exotic ones: Turkey, Morocco, China, the Greek Islands, Bangkok, Bali and Singapore. Trips that were not always easy. Most of the countries were hot, and she felt the heat, but she trouped, and my affection for her continued to ascend. I was filled with admiration for her, coupled with worry that the strain might be too much. She never complained, never asked for things, never wasted words, and ended each trip with, "I think I'd like to go on the next one."

On our last trip together, we went to the Czech Republic, Hungary, Austria and Poland. She didn't feel well one evening in Vienna, and I worried. She told me she just needed to rest. Sure enough, the next day she seemed okay. Then, toward the end of the trip, while walking in the square in Crakow, she said, "Bob, I don't know what's the matter with me; I don't seem to be able to keep up." She was perspiring heavily, and my worry grew. I walked with her, as I had always tried to do, anyway, and though she appeared to be all right for the short remainder of the trip and enjoyed the festivities of our final evening in a tavern in Warsaw, where we had an evening of folkloric dancing and singing with our dinner, I was unable to relax.

The trip ended with no problems, and Grace mentioned merely that she might be getting too old. I felt a darkness.

Six months later I learned she had passed away. There are relatives whose passing did not affect me as Grace's did. I continue to think of her more often than I would imagine, and it's been a few years now. Her round face, with the heavy eye glasses and the braided blondish hair are always a clear image.

I miss that sweet, sweet lady. Often, in my mind's eye, I see her pausing to take a quick rest and then following with her recognizable gait with the cane. Sweet face. Sweet Grace.

WHO'S AFRAID OF VIRGINIA ?

Somerset Maugham, the well-traveled English novelist, once stated that most people are so ugly, the least they could do is to be pleasant in order to make up for it.

Virginia had thick blue-black hair worn in Perry Winkle style. It could break a rake. Her nose was bulbous, and she had ostrich skin. She was referred to me by a cousin of hers who had been on a couple of my trips and who recommended me highly. She wanted to room with Virginia on this upcoming trip, but Virginia refused. Moreover, Virginia could not attend the orientation. A bad omen.

I sent Virginia as much information as I could and spoke to her a couple of times by phone. Her cousin assured me she would also fill her in on details. The next step was to meet her at the airport.

Everyone else was on time at the airport and checked in. No sign of Virginia. Her cousin told me not to worry, but she did not remain with me to help me identify this person I had never seen. Departure time was nearing, and there was still no Virginia. Finally she arrived, appearing totally unconcerned about being tardy. I checked my worries as the plane ascended and headed for Turkey, a favorite of the many countries I had visited. I was as eager as my fellow travelers, totally unaware that I could expect some serious trouble from my tardy passenger.

As scheduled, we stayed in Ankara only for overnight, at a most impressive Hilton hotel. Departure the next morning was extremely early because of an early flight to Cappadocia, where we were to spend the next few days. Virginia complained loudly that she didn't get up that early at home and resented having to do so here. One of the other women mentioned that the schedule was included in the brochure.

I try routinely, perhaps foolishly, to note whether everything is okay with all people at all times, but somehow I did not pick up on the fact that, as the trip progressed, Virginia was not mixing well. Others, however, sensed this early on, and I learned through them that she disliked the food, the restaurants and the fact that we weren't meeting "the natives."

Cappadocia fascinates everyone, with its caves created by the ancient Christians as secret places to worship when their worship was forbidden; the fairy chimneys shaped by the peculiar erosion formation of the mountains; the fantasy look of the cotton candy castles of petrified lime in Pammukale. To travel from Cappadocia westward required lengthy overland motorcoaching. It meant one long bus ride upon return to the western section of the area we were visiting. But only one.

Ladies on the bus spoke of Virginia's constant "bitching" about the long ride. She complained that we should have been flying instead. Correctly, the ladies told her you cannot fly where there is no airport, and since there was only one real day of excessive overland travel, why not try to appreciate the unique and remarkable landscape? Virginia concentrated instead on the agony of traveling with thirty people, mostly women, which made the ladies ask why she had signed on for a group trip in the first place if she disliked traveling with a group.

We spent a few hours in Ephesus, walking through the splendid ruins, which were about as complete for an ancient Roman city as one could find anywhere. Though there is never enough time in a place you love, the visit was thorough and full. Some time later, Virginia complained that there was not enough time there. Yet, when we visited the Blue Mosque in Istanbul, where there really was limited time, she never shut up while the guide was explaining what everyone was there to learn.

On a previous trip to this enchanting land, I had not been able to work in a visit to Perge, Side and Aspendos. This time I was insistent on getting them in, especially Aspendos, with that not-to-be-believed theater. It was on the day of that special visit that Virginia decided to take the day off and have her hair done. Others on the trip wished she could have done something about her personality instead. Virginia afterwards said that was a most enjoyable day for her; the rest of the group said it was more enjoyable for *them*.

Someone asked the guide how much our magnificent Mercedes motorcoach cost. He answered, "About a half million dollars. That's more than the cost of some of your homes, isn't it?"

Virginia took offense at that, as if it had been a personal attack. When, early in the trip, the guide had mentioned that there was a toilet on board, but asked that we use it only in emergencies because of the possible odors, Virginia said he was being a dictator, not allowing us the use of the toilet at all. On almost every motorcoach anywhere, the guide makes the announcement that this guide had made. I have never known anyone to misunderstand or be upset. It's logical, after all.

Virginia complained that we did not have enough time for lunch, although we usually had at *least* an hour and a half. She also hated the food, in spite of its great variety. And she objected to small paper napkins, wanting, instead, linen ones.

She wanted to have more time to wander among the people of Turkey. Our outstanding young Turkish guide was, by everyone else's taste, one of the best we had ever had. Virginia never got to know him. She did not like the idea of eating with a group. This was a group tour at a remarkably low group price in spite of the high standards of guide, motorcoach, hotels, itinerary etc., but she resented the group idea. Why in hell did she take a group tour? She was making everyone hate her. If she wanted to go off on her own, she obviously should have taken a trip on her own. She did not like having a schedule; she did not like being with a group; she did not like the food; she did not like having to get up in the morning. She had no good words. She condemned almost everything that everyone else loved.

She did admit later that she had not read the brochure very carefully beforehand. With forked tongue, she used the trip as a sounding board for her misery, wherever that had come from. She was unrealistic, unfair and unjustified. She was, as the others labeled her, a bitch.

Screw you, Madame DeFarge.

JO, THE BLONDIES AND TEXAS

When you're a teacher, it's impossible not to favor some students over others. You can't show it or play favorites, but you cannot deny to yourself that some students are just more winning than others. Well, why should it be any different in travel? You want all your clients to be like the best ones you know, but that cannot be, and you must go along, seeming to feel equally about all.

I link Jo, the blondies and Texas because they usually travel together, they're unique, and though they're all individual, I cannot think of one without my thoughts segueing into the others.

Jo was a student in my Marymount class and has traveled with me since the first trip to Egypt. She's tall, and her goodness is as tall as she is. I cannot imagine that she could have a negative thought. She's plagued with physical problems that would defeat the average person, but she's determined to make the best of everything, and she does it with dauntless skill. She never does anything to draw attention, but she always enjoys watching someone else get it when the reason is positive.

In Jo's class at Marymount was an opposite: Mamie, the first of the two blondes, who caused and enjoyed attention, being unbridled, uninhibited and ready for whatever fun was available. Though she had grown children, she looked about the age of her own children. A good sport with a ready smile, Mamie was always where the fun was and always had the best of times. She was divorced long before I ever knew her, and I still see her only as energy personified. When anyone in the group was laughing, if it wasn't Mamie, Mamie was nearby. She just had fun wherever she went, and it was infectious.

Especially in Third World countries where blondes were special just for being blond, the men were always aware of Mamie. I remember, on that Egypt trip, having to step in at a small airport where some soldiers were closing in on her, and I worried that I had no camels with which to counter any offers they might make for her.

Bootsie came along on that first trip with Mamie, and she, too, shocked me with the knowledge that she had a couple of children in their teens. Could she have had them when she was a kindergartener?

In the beginning, Mamie and Bootsie seemed pretty much of the same personality, but as the years passed and I learned more about them from successive trips, I saw how different they were, Bootsie seeming more and more like the more serious of the two. But in the beginning, they just seemed like two girls without responsibility, out to enjoy whatever there was to enjoy, never resting, never less than raring to go. They giggled and laughed and had fun throughout the trip, with no apparent worries or cares. And shopping! They bought everything! When hawkers approached at historical sites and the crowd tried to shoo them off, the two blondies always found something to buy. When the bus stopped en route and hawkers tried to vend, they had easy marks in those two. They bought beads and trinkets and souvenirs till their luggage squeaked. I often joke that when the bus stopped for a traffic light, they found it possible to get off, buy something and get back on before the light changed. The whole crowd laughed, and of course everyone knew who they were. We wondered if the venders had a system to alert other venders ahead to prepare for two blondes. The rest of us stopped watching the sites and started watching the buying ritual.

After a couple of years, Texas came into Bootsie's life, and they traveled together, while Jo and Mamie doubled up. He was a young guy who was as casual as could be, and he and Bootsie made a super couple, always spending their time with Jo and Mamie. And he was one of those good guys who would always be on hand to help an older traveler with luggage or up and down the stairs.

He was a silent hero you could always count on, though he would have shunned credit if it was offered. Bootsie was quieter with Texas than with Mamie, and they often gave the impression of a couple who'd been together all their lives, the way only much older people do.

The four friends were together on most trips from the time Texas entered the picture, and I realized that I felt something missing when they could not take a particular trip. It was my good fortune that they took most trips I ran.

Each was quite different from the other three, but they worked perfectly together, and I'm better for having them in my life. And in the past couple of years, Bootsie's two fine sons have been with us, the only "younger" travelers we've had, and it's been a special treat to see the sites through the eyes of these two extraordinary young men, now in their early twenties. They, too, were always on hand to aid an older person, and they were always proper and admirable wherever we went and whatever we did. Sometimes I would stop watching the subject matter in order to enjoy the look of appreciation on their faces as they absorbed these worlds that were new and exciting to them. If we arrived at a ruin with high peaks, in a matter of seconds they were on the top. If there was a stray dog outside a hotel, they never forgot to take orts from the table.

Somewhere during each trip, Jo would manage to say, "Bob, I'm having a wonderful time," or "This is great." I know she did that to assure me that all was what I'd wanted it to be. I was never able to relax about the success of a trip. Regina often said that if there were twenty-five students in my class, and twenty-four were successful, I could not relax because I hadn't gotten that one student who didn't make it. So it was with the trips. I needed to feel that everyone was having the best time of his life. That's a sure sign of failure, right off the bat. How could any normal person hope to please all the people all the time? Ridiculous! Well, Jo's mission was to assure me that all was okay.

She talked easily and enthusiastically, but she was essentially quiet, taking beautiful photos with a wonderful camera. She never latched on to anyone, though friendly with all, but, rather, she absorbed the sites and the lectures and photographed unobtrusively. Her own records of the trips were thoughtful and insightful.

All four were in their early forties when we started. Jo made the perfect companion for whomever she roomed with, constantly helpful and congenial, though never one to have to be linked. She was always where she should be, on time, totally accepting about everything, from the hotel room to tours, to shopping times, to food. If I had to illustrate the perfect traveler, Jo would get my vote.

When Bootsie began traveling with Texas, and Jo began rooming with Mamie, I often wondered how their opposite identities might meld. Well, they did. Mamie would be the first one to praise Jo's great nature, and Jo would be easily able to say that Mamie's fun-loving nature was a lift. Jo provided a fine audience for Mamie's uninhibitiveness. In a cafe in an evening, Mamie would laugh wildly at something; Jo would smile her silent smile. Never an unkind thought between them.

As we traveled more and more, I learned that Bootsie took her own brand of notes, and each evening she religiously transposed them into solid, refined form. During all flights she read. I'm a fine traveler, but, as I've mentioned, I don't sleep on a plane because I can only sleep face down. If I glanced around the darkened cabin on a long flight and noticed one reading light on, it would be Bootsie's. She traveled with several books, and all travel time was spent reading them, and she finished all. I never learned whether it was coincidence or influence, but Texas and Bootsie's boys did the same.

People began to notice that Bootsie was quite the shopper. She bought quality items at high prices. She bought things others admired but thought were too costly. As one who does more than his share of buying large, cumbersome, costly irresistibles myself, I must say I admire her taste. Bootsie owns her own company, employing a large staff. It stuns people upon learning that, because her appearance is so young.

I've watched Texas do his own purchasing. Every now and again I see him musing over some handmade item, and he adds to his own collection of memorabilia, again with special admirable taste. There is a slight smile that is a part of his countenance that widens when you admire his purchase.

Even the boys: they don't buy often, but some unique, sometimes nicely grotesque thing that represents the place for them, and they make a special choice for the one thing that brings the country home with them. As something of an onlooker, this is all warming to watch.

I know Mamie well enough to have asked her how she's managed to remain single. Her reply is simply that the right guy just isn't around. An obvious answer to an obvious question, but there isn't the obvious frustration. Maybe it's because she has been married and does have adult children, but I think she's comfortable enough to be able to have a good time, which many women in her circumstance don't allow themselves. She never frets, so her joie de vivre becomes infectious, and you have fun because she does. There's some kind of gift in that.

Jo's attitude is to get the most from every situation, so she does. I've never known anyone to derive so much pleasure from other people's happiness, but she genuinely does. Without a single false note, each person's good fortune apparently provides her with the same pleasure she would feel if she were the direct recipient. She truly is the personification of the word "friend", and one is better for having her in his life. There is a precious quality in her. She has so much to be bitter about, and she radiates only happiness.

So this group remains to this day set apart in a golden spot of my life. If all went wrong, but they were on hand, the situation would be fine. How gratifying to have had the luxury of their company on many, many trips. They alone have made them worthwhile.

SUZANNE

Suzanne found me the way Grace had found me. She had been coming on the weekend trips, and now she wanted to come to foreign territory. She was in her sixties, but she looked a decade younger, although she was badly crippled with rheumatoid arthritis to the extent that one leg did not bend at all and the other required her to walk on only the ball of her foot. She used a cane. Her fingers were gnarled, but she had a beautiful handwriting. Her face showed a permanent strain from her condition, as if arthritis ran through it as well. It was easy to see that at one time she had been quite pretty. She had pale blond hair and large, expressive eyes, and as soon as she spoke you knew she was intelligent.

Suzanne did not mingle on the trips. She walked alone, in her dragging gait, and was always at the rear of the group when they walked. But she caught up and never complained. She could never adjust the speed with which she walked. She did not apologize or ask for favors. She made certain that she knew the departure time each day, and then she would be the first one to breakfast in order not to have to be waited for. She always got to the bus early; she was unable to get on or off without assistance, but that was almost the only assistance she would accept.

She became friendly with and trusting of Regina, and through Regina I learned of some awkwardnesses of the handicapped that I might not have known otherwise. For example, when using a public toilet, Regina would go in ahead of time in order to arrange for the use of toilet paper because Suzanne was unable to grasp it in the new, large dispensers which often require that one bend far in order to retrieve it. I think of that every single time I cannot start the roll easily.

She always took a single room, and I always worried about her slipping in the tub or shower. Through Regina I learned that she almost always sponge-bathed on the trips. She would not enter a tub and could use a shower only if the stall was easily accessible.

At a table she could not sit up straight; she angled into a chair and remained that way, getting the food to her mouth with awkwardness, or what would be awkwardness to others; she was used to it. Everywhere people watched her with amazement. She managed to maneuver through situations that seemed impossible.

Her voice was very strong, her speech showed breeding. She told me long after we had met that she had been married to an army officer who had left after her illness, which had begun in college, had accelerated. She was not remorseful or angry or bitter. She did not dramatize or embellish. When asked what she did for a living, she would answer that she was a secretary. Because one assumed she had a position of high power the next question was generally, "What kind of secretary?" Her answer was, "Just a secretary."

She did drive—a regular car with hand controls but without a special seat. She was totally independent.

Suzanne never looked for friendships on the trips, as many people do. She came for the itinerary, and that would have been enough. And of course she did not want anything that resembled pity.

After having done a number of my weekend trips, and learning how I operate, she told me she would like to go to Turkey if I thought she could do it. She was quick to say that if there were places that were inaccessible for her or where she might hold everyone up, I was to tell her beforehand. Branded in my memory is her statement: "If I only get to do half of it, it would be twice as much as if I didn't go at all."

She was, of course, able to get airport assistance, a wheelchair and luggage handling, plus a bulkhead seat to allow for the leg that did not bend. Even when a flight could not accommodate that, she made the best of her discomfort.

Each day in Turkey, a difficult trip for a first-timer, she asked how long the walk would be from the end of a visit to the bus, and then she would see to it that she allowed herself enough time to leave the visit early and get to the bus before the group in order that they not have to wait for her. Most of the time, the driver would lift her off the bus, rather than have her struggle. She weighed nothing, and in the beginning *I* lifted her off, but she soon learned I have a bad back and she refused my help. I know she always tipped the driver extra at the end of the trip.

She traveled well and presented no problems. She thanked me for "taking her". Everyone admired her guts. Except for climbing the snowy mountains in Cappadocia, she did pretty much the whole trip. Though she obviously did not climb the steps of the theaters, she did walk all through Ephesus and Hieropolis and a dozen other wearing sites. Stairs were her nemesis, and there was always someone who reached out an arm to assist. But she was a marvel, and having done Turkey, the world was open to her. We did several trips together.

In particular I remember our trip to Morocco. Upon arrival in the airport in Casablanca, she said, "I've lost my return ticket!" I spent the remainder of the trip faxing each day to Air Moroc in New York, trying to get her a return ticket. They insisted she would have to buy another round trip ticket, the cost for the first half to be refunded in six months. I kept pleading with them just to reissue her return half; I explained her condition. It was an impossible task. The whole trip was ruined for me because I kept worrying about Suzanne.

This was the shortest trip I had ever done—eight days. On the sixth day, when I received from the States the same stumbling-block reply about the ticket and showed my exasperation, I almost got exasperated at Suzanne as well because she said, "Bob, I don't know why you're so upset. I'm not. They're certainly not going to make me stay here."

I did not have her comfort of mind. Fortunately, on the seventh day, the fax reply said the ticket situation was taken care of, and all ended well.

Suzanne subsequently came with us to Southern France and to Southern Italy and Sicily. Meeting new people each time, she impressed ever more meople with her courage, and strangers would remark to me, "What a soldier she is."

A month after our return from Sicily, in the fall of '96, I received a call from a sorority sister of Suzanne, telling me Suzanne was in a New York hospital, having suffered from an aneurism. I tried to contact her in order to visit, but only family was allowed, and Suzanne had only two relatives, a distant aunt and cousin. I called the hospital almost daily for a report. It was difficult to get any real information.

Then, after a couple of weeks, the answer to my call was that Suzanne "had expired." As I write the words, I re-experience the sinking of my heart.

At her funeral, the pastor mentioned Suzanne's love of travel and what these recent trips had meant. She had told him so much of this last trip to Sicily and what joy it had given her. I was unable to hold back the tears.

IRA AND ETHEL

When a couple is special, that makes it extra special, because you luck out twice. So it was with Ira and Ethel, deserving of the Couple of the Year award in travel.

Ira was a robust, hearty guy with a round, red face that was always smiling. Behind his glasses sparkled mischievous eyes, and he always had a joke for the moment. Ira always wore Bermudas and bright suspenders; if we dressed at all for dinner, he wore a bow tie.

Ethel enjoyed all her husband's jokes and ways. When she smiled, and she always smiled, her eyes closed. She listened intently when anyone spoke, and if there was a joke at the end, she broke into laughter that made her eyes tear.

Both had pure white hair, and they were never apart. They were the first ones on the dance floor, and others lit up just by watching them. They never had the need to be the center of attention, yet one wanted to center attention on them. Everyone referred to them as "cute." They were in the middle of all activity and seemed to liven the atmosphere through their own innate electricity. You could pick them out as the typical American couple. They looked typical and they looked American–in the best possible way. They were just a pair you always wanted in your company.

We did many trips together, and each time their reservation arrived in the mail, I felt a special lift, because their company automatically meant a good time. They were jolly and energetic and interested. They mixed well, and everyone looked forward to their company. Their enjoyment was infectious. They were the perfect travelers.

After some years, Ira developed Parkinson's. On each trip it was a little worse. Ethel treated him wonderfully. As time went on, the progression of the disease took its toll on Ira's speech, and he became more and more difficult to understand. It pained me to have to ask him to repeat, because I knew it registered with him that I had difficulty understanding, and that would spotlight his condition. I didn't want to embarrass him as I cringed for him.

Time came when his walking was stiffened and halting. He walked in what seemed to be a metered gait. This strong and lively man was set back to a state which had to bear a heavy toll. Gone was the time when he could crack a funny joke impromptu; gone were the dancing times. Over and over in a day I was distracted by thoughts of him, this terrific guy now having such difficulty with simple everyday things.

At the conclusion of the last trip orientation, after I had announced that I was going to be giving up tour leading, Ira, on his way out, mumbled something I could not understand. Hesitantly I asked him to repeat.

"If you're not leading any more trips," he said, "I'm not taking any more." Tears rolled down his face.

I hugged the guy and murmured only, "Oh, Ira."

The minute he got out the door, I broke down.

Knowing the sickness is half the cure.

Sometimes I'm asked by travel companies to lead a tour of theirs. I honestly don't remember how I got started in that, but several times a year I would get a call to ask if I would host a trip. That means being tour guide/tour manager/trouble shooter. I enjoy it. It's a different sense of responsibility. I still feel totally responsible for the people, who are all strangers to me, but if there's something about the trip they don't like, I don't take it personally, because the creation of it wasn't mine. I feel for their unhappiness, but I don't feel burdened or liable. They would have to blame the company: they understand that, and it's easier all around.

I led a two-week ethnic tour of central Europe. The design of the tour, with what was included, was excellent, but most meals were not included, and I prefer to include them. This was a group that, for the most part, was accepting of the idea of being on their own for meals.

The most miserable of all on the trip was Carol, a woman traveling alone. She was socially inept and naturally disagreeable. I thought again of W. Somerset Maugham's statement to the effect that "some people are so ugly, the least they could do is be pleasant, to make up for it." When I introduced myself at the airport, she asked, "Who are you?" as I was telling her. The company did goof. They neglected to tell this group they were having an American host with them. That made it extremely uncomfortable for me, because, though I was appreciated, I know they had to think, "Here's someone else to have to tip." I wish that embarrassment on no one. Carol also said at the start, to Regina, who was with me on this one, "Who needs him?"

The first day in Prague, we were taken on a tour which ended in the town square, from which we had to find our way back to the hotel on our own. I told the company that that planning is poor. This woman had to find a place for dinner the first night and get back, without knowing anyone. Everyone else in the group was traveling with a mate or companion. During the flight and the arrival at the hotel, which also necessitated a long wait for the rooms, and a waste of time (which I also reported to the company), the others in the group had decided this woman, Carol, was to be avoided. This room wait should have been supplanted with the city tour that occurred later. The arrival was too early to check in; there was nothing to do in the hotel; the company knew this; it should have arranged for the bags to be checked in without the group waiting, and then they could have had the tour, been returned to the hotel, which they were not, and all would have been fine.

Back to Carol, one could not help but have the feeling she had planned not to be happy. She complained about everything in a gravelly voice, often followed by a hacking smoker's cough. She must have used one match a day, never being without a cigarette. Many people avoided her for that; she had no regard for people's comfort at dinner tables or elsewhere. Fortunately, she did not have to be asked not to smoke inside visited sites or on the bus. But she commented negatively throughout the trip, grumbling whether or not she was listened to, and no one wanted to be in her company. There semed to be nothing she liked. Normally, a person traveling alone is asked by others to join them at dinner; there is always someone who invites. Not so here, and understandably. Regina and I certainly would have seen to it that Carol was not left. Impossible. Even making perfunctory conversation was an effort. Of all the dislikeable people who ever turned up on a trip, I guess she was the worst. She was hateful.

On our introductory ride from the airport to the hotel, the guide routinely, but pleasantly, asked if anyone had been to the Czech Republic before. One man, Moe, said loudly, "Eighty times." Throughout the trip, in his over-resonant voice, he added to whatever the guide said. I never knew anyone so eager to share his knowledge. It was so regular, it was torture. You knew he considered himself to be bright, but how could he not have thought somewhere along the line that he was overdoing it? I don't know if anyone cared at all for his comments.

His wife, Verna, was a travel agent who told me every day how outstanding I was. I don't think it took three days before I realized this wasn't praise; she was greasing me up. They hadn't finalized their plans for an extension at the end of the trip, and she wanted me to help her with those arrangements. She should have been better-equipped than I to take care of it. All it involved was getting transportation to the train station and getting their luggage aboard. As a travel agent, that should have been a snap.

Moe mentioned a few times during the trip that he overtips. When the trip was over and he gave me an envelope, I assure you it was no overtip.

Two women in every way opposite of the others were Connie and Max(ine). They should never have come together. Connie was about sixty, an ebullient talker who wanted everyone to hear everything she ever had to say. If she was telling a story, and someone else came near, she would call that person over and begin anew. If, then, another person came by, she would do the same thing, so that the first listener would hear regular retellings. She perspired profusely and always spoke with great enthusiasm, regardless of subject. Her nature was marvelous–friendly, giving, helpful. But she was rather much. The attention she required for endless stories she insisted on telling was grating.

Max, fortyish, was small and tough, with red hair that was cropped like a boy's. Much of what she said seemed to come out of the side of her mouth, and one had the impression that she was a member of a motorcycle gang. She even had a tattoo on her shoulder. She looked like a female skinhead. That these two were roommates provided a trip-long query.

Early on, it seemed there would be trouble between them. Max made faces when Connie expounded. She also muttered about her, and it seemed quite a while before Connie picked up on that. "Man, does she go on," Max would groan. As the days passed they were less and less, if at all, together. Max's grumbling was glowing embers panting for dry wood. But she grumbled about many things–and people–so maybe it was not aimed just at Connie. At one point, in the Jewish Cemetery in Prague, she was overheard to say, "Can you believe how many Jews are on this trip?"

Before our three-day stay in Budapest came to an end, the two women were having difficulty. By the time we reached Vienna, our next stop, there was definite trouble.

The group seemed to average in the seventies in age except for Connie and Max and two couples who became friendly in the first few days, after deciding that they, in their early fifties, might hit it off together. Husband number one had to be waited for every morning while everyone sat on the bus. I had to tell him each time. One day it was because he left his sweater; another time he had to use the bathroom; another time he was kept waiting at the cashier's desk; once he "just hadn't finished breakfast." Each day there was a different excuse, but nevertheless we would have to wait. Each day I would tell him the next day we'd have to leave without him if he was late; each next day his wife would say, "But he'll be right here." He never apologized, never looked bothered, never quickened his step.

His wife complained that the fish at the restaurant did not taste like home. Regina and I are still trying to work out a non-obvious comeback for that one, one that does not have the word ROME in it or the word IF.

Wife number two, upon checking into each new hotel and going to her room, would appear at the desk and demand a room on a higher floor. If the hotel had eight floors and she was on seven, she demanded to be put on eight; if the hotel had twelve floors and she was on eleven, she demanded to be on twelve. It takes a while before I get to my room, because after I give out the keys and everyone goes to their rooms, there is always paper work for me or details to be worked out with the new guide. So before I ever left the lobby, I got to know that wife number 2 would appear with her regular request. I do say I enjoyed it when she was turned down—for whatever reason. When, after the second or third visit, the two wives appeared, I realized she'd pulled her new friend in on her plan.

Several people in the group complained about prices everywhere, whether the prices seemed high or not. But there was the woman who insisted on going to Herend to buy, though I did not see a purchase, and the couple who had to go to the Sachar Hotel for a Sachar torte. Herend is a store which sells the ultimate in quality items, whatever they are; the Sachar Hotel is romantically elegant in the grand sense; and a Sachar torte is a rich pastry for which diners pant. There was a couple who came with a seventeen-page itinerary laid out by the wife's sister, telling her what she must take in. We would have an old hotel pointed out to us as an historical landmark, and this wife would say, "They're supposed to have the best restaurant in the city." If the guide left us in a public square, where there were historical sites not to be missed, she would either ask how to get to a particular restaurant or ask where the best one was. I had recommended a restaurant I especially enjoy in the town square in Crakow, but it was not expensive enough.

One night we were going to a concert in Budapest. The concert hall was a block from our hotel. There is a charming restaurant within spitting distance of the hall, complete with roving violinist (how much more Hungarian can you get?), but they'd heard of a particular restaurant across the city, requiring a taxi ride and extra expense, and that did it. But when it came to making a purchase they complained over the difference in pennies: "You can get that for less three blocks from here."

And we all know the people who take rolls or cake from the breakfast table to serve as lunch later on. These gourmands took part in that.

Arrival in a new city prompted them to ask loudly about tickets to the opera or the ballet or anything that would impress the others with their culture. Verna had told us many times about their hundred-and-fifty-dollar tickets to the opera in Vienna. Yuk.

In Vienna, Connie, who now had a bad cold, called me one evening to say it was so difficult with Max, she wanted to leave for home when the rest of us went on to Poland. I told her it would be expensive to make that change with the airlines.

"I don't care about not getting a refund for the Poland portion of the trip," she said. "I just can't continue this way. She's making it much too unpleasant."

"But your fare home was based on a group plan. They'll apply a penalty, I'm sure."

"I don't care," she answered. "I want to get out of here. It has nothing to do with you or the trip; I just want out."

"How about trying for a single room instead?" I suggested. It will be expensive, but still cheaper than a switch in flights."

"I just can't continue," she replied.

"I understand," I said. And I did. "I cannot call the airlines for you, though. There will have to be many questions they will ask that I cannot answer for you."

She called the airlines, and there were no flights available. "I'll have to make the best of it," she told me. "I'm a big girl. I'll get through it."

And so she did. Their relationship seemed to improve, then stagger, then level off. They did survive each other.

One of the visits was to the salt mines in Crakow. They are as impressive as anything can be, with all the carvings done out of the walls of salt. To visit the full-sized cathedral, there, where every bit, including chandeliers, is made of salt, takes one's breath. After the visit, I had to ask the group how they enjoyed it, and the comments were monosyllabic. I remembered how, when describing a meal they had just had, however, they counted the number of peas and described the thickness of the cut and the flakiness of the crust and the texture of the salad. It was a form of torture to be with this group.

The woman who had her sister's itinerary had requested an aisle seat on the return flight because she had a bad leg which needed no attention while we traveled up, down and around, but which needed a special seat on the plane. She put in the request, she said, several days before we left, and she called from the hotel desk on the day of departure. When we arrived at the airport, her request was not granted. She came over to me and complained. She was one who'd put in requests on the trip, such as one-hour detours to places not in the intinerary, and never said a word of thanks when they were fulfilled. I went to the desk with her and her husband and told the attendant the request had been made in advance and that the couple did expect the special seating. The attendant said it was impossible. We left the desk. Five minutes later, the attendant approached me and said she was granting the request to the couple but wanted *me* to tell them; it was because of their attitude that she'd refused, but she wanted me to know that she was giving it to them because of me. When I told the couple they were getting their request, there again was no thank you.

That trip, that group, was an exception. While there's a bad apple in almost every barrel, I'd never had a group like that. Certainly my own have never been that way, but even all those I've led for travel companies have not been like this one. They were, somehow, all the worst stereotypes.

It was the only time I led a group of strangers with Regina; it was the only time I avoided them at mealtimes. I've always socialized with the group and gone where they've gone to eat. Though there were a few sweet people in the group– and I do mean a few–Regina and I were by ourselves for most of the "free" time.

Redundancy on the part of a teacher may just be a handicap born of the constant need to emphasize.

I arrived in LAX (Los Angeles Airport) at 6:30 P.M. for our midnight flight to Fiji. At the check-in counter I immediately learned they would not process until 8:30. I was happy my luggage had been ticketed all the way through so that I wouldn't have to be stuck with it now. I began to search for the strangers I would be leading on this trip. They were told to wear the travel company's identification badges to enable me to find them; I, in turn, wore one as well.

We were flying Air Pacific, a kind of partner of Qantas. The Qantas counter was busy, but Air Pacific, at the very next counter, could not process the gathering people for our flight. As various people approached the counter, each walked away with the same message: nothing could be done until 8:30. The incoming plane that would take us would be late, so our flight, accordingly, would be late.

By 8:00 the people for our flight began to form a line, and I watched for the familiar company badges. Though people came without them, I approached some when I spotted the matching luggage tags. They had no difficulty putting the tags on the bags, but some were reluctant to wear the ones that would tell me who they were.

I had misgivings about leading this trip. The man who owned and ran the company knew me from previous trips I had led for a large company he had worked for in the past. I had done trips of my own, using the previous company's itineraries (which the company enjoyed because I had acquired all the passengers myself, from my own mailing list), and I had led trips for the company, as well, meaning that I served as a tour host (or guide or leader or manager) for trips I neither designed nor recruited for.

Why was I doing this?–Because, as I've said, I don't really have to recruit, I don't have to design the itinerary, I won't have the same sense of over-responsibility I feel when I do the whole thing myself. I will not have picked the touring sites, the hotels, the eating places, and if someone doesn't like something, they'll know it was not my design. I would work no less diligently, but I would not feel the same sense of despair if a hotel did not suit someone. Hopefully it won't be like the European trip of imperfect strangers.

I did send out a newsletter, and a handful of my mailing list responded. As in the past with Australia and New Zealand, the trip came in December, and I never plan my own trips for that month, regardless of the destination. As it turned out, most of my followers who wanted this trip to this place were not able to come anyway because of the bad time of year. Had I known that to begin with, I would not have considered going in the first place, but now I had obligated myself to both the company and those who had signed on.

So here I was in LAX, as the line to the check-in counter swelled.

The first group I met was a Rumanian couple with their pretty daughter, about thirty. Mother and daughter wore more makeup than I ever saw off the stage. It was dramatically, theatrically effective, but unusual to see for a trip. Bela, the husband, began by telling me that he did not like the idea that flying from Fiji into Cairns, Australia, had a stopover in Brisbane. "That's just to save the company money," he stated gruffly, in his heavy accent. "I'm going to tell them that," he said.

I wasn't too sure of the purpose in that stop, myself, but I guessed, "I think it's more expensive to make the stop. It requires more services. However, it's an international airport, and that's our arrival into Australia. That's probably the reason." I hoped I defended the company honorably.

"It's not a good idea. We just waste time that way. We should go straight to Cairns. And if this flight from L.A. is going to be late, how do we get back the time we will lose? I don't like this already. How are they going to make up for that? What do you think about that?"

What I thought about it was that this is one of those damnable questions that can arise. Most people are reasonable enough to accept that unhappy occurrence. Experience has taught me that the person who aggravates about that will be on my back about a dozen other things, as well. I could already tell that Bela would be demanding and possibly relentless. Sheez, we hadn't left yet.

Wife and daughter smiled all the while, as Bela told me how he researched trips on the computer and knew how to get the best prices. I know the attraction to this particular trip was its price. Under $2500, it included eight flights, first class hotels, full buffet breakfasts, many tours, superb buses and drivers, porterage and many details. True, lunches and dinners were not included, and many tours were optional, meaning that to take them meant to pay extra for them. But with all the extras, the trip was far below the cost of any others to the same areas, and it was a two-and-a-half-week trip. I had done almost the same trip before, and though more tours were included, the price was considerably higher. This trip was, in every sense of the word, a bargain.

I did not worry especially about Bela and his family. Hopefully, the trip would prove itself and so would I. I knew he was evaluating me, so I asked him what grade he was giving me to start with. "C+," he answered.

"I guess I have to work on my term paper," I replied.

The next group I met held fewer prospects. A couple in their seventies, traveling with their unhappy ten-year-old granddaughter, invaded the three-and-four-abreast waiting line of more than a hundred people, oblivious to the frowns of those around them. Instead of getting on the end of the line, they managed to place themselves about a quarter of the way from the front. Somehow they got away with it.

Upon meeting passengers, it is my habit to check with them about their luggage, being sure they have just one check-in piece and one acceptable carry-on. Estelle, the wife, told me they had four pieces of check-in, but that it was all right because they were allowed two apiece. I informed her they were only allowed one check-in apiece. She insisted they could have two apiece. After one more volley, I produced the letter each passenger was sent, which clearly stated one was the amount. She insisted she would take the extra one regardless. I told her it was fine with me, but if the airlines charged her for it, there would be nothing I could do. The international flights did not present a problem, but the internal ones might.

Next, I noticed she had a roll-on carry-on, which this airline did not accept as a carry-on. This, too, had been clearly stated in the documents each passenger had received from the travel company. That message was given in order to prevent the problem of people assuming that any roll-on carry-on is automatically accepted by any airline. Since it was emphasized in the documents, everyone knew ahead of time, and no one else brought that particular bag as a carry-on.

When boarding time did arrive (and I'm jumping the gun in time in this case), Estelle was told she could not take the bag onto the plane. I stood by as she argued with the airline personnel, telling them the dimensions of the bag, while they proved it did not fit into the framework arranged for that exact purpose. Although the bag clearly did not fit, she continuously repeated its dimensions. People around her were telling her the rules, the airlines personnel told her, and she heard not.

Her voice was very shrill and strident, and the angrier she got, the shriller and more strident that voice became. Strangers showed their disgust, and she remained oblivious.

Finally she stated that her husband's medication was in the bag and he would need it. They asked her to remove the medication and they would provide a suitable bag for it. She asserted that they needed it all. They softly told her they would provide a bag that would fit in the overhead compartment. When she said her own (unacceptable) bag was filled with medication, everyone shared the thought that if that bag was filled with medication, there would be enough for all of Australia.

The airline personnel could not and therefore did not give in. Estelle begrudgingly, poutingly, furiously opened her carry-on and removed items of clothing that filled the largest part of the bag, and, finally, placed the medication into a provided, much smaller, bag, losing not only her argument but her credibility. It had been such a waste of time. In the airport, all she had to do was to accept what I had told her. That's one of the reasons I'm on a trip. All the pain could have been avoided.

While in line, back in the airport (and back in the proper sequence of events), her husband told me he cannot stand for long periods of time and did not want to wait in line. I suggested he sit on his luggage. He told me that would not be comfortable. "Since we're in for a long wait," I said, "maybe you would prefer to wait in one of the comfortable lounge chairs up ahead. They're not far away, and you could relax while your wife and granddaughter stay with the luggage. The line is not moving anyway."

"No," he answered. "I don't want to leave them here."

I was unable to come up with another suggestion.

Seeing these three off were the granddaughter's parents. The father, who had not introduced himself, told me, "My daughter is not waiting in any line. Get her to the gate area where she can lie down! It's late!"

"No one even knows yet which gate we'll be using," I said. "We don't know when the plane is coming in yet."

"This airline sucks! The company is using it just to save money," he countered. "I'm going to sue, and I'm going to take my daughter off the trip, and they're going to refund my money!"

Why did you pick this company or this trip, I wondered.

Did the cost you're talking about have some little something to do with that?

"Everybody wants to get checked in. They're all impatient. But it isn't the fault of the company OR the airline. However, if you want to take your daughter off the trip, that's up to you."

"Well, she's not standing here till that plane takes off, I can tell you that!"

People in the immediate area, whose space these people had invaded in the first place, began to murmur and state that they were not enjoying the wait, either, but what could you do? These things happen in airports. And the line kept building. The father heard nothing or was able to dismiss it all brilliantly. He was identifiably Jewish, and that fact became part of the dialog. Being Jewish and caring very much about the stereotypical negativism that can incur, I felt the discomfort I have felt in other, similar situations. It is not that the same situation couldn't occur with a cast of non-Jewish characters; the fact is that these were Jews, and I'm a Jew, and I was uncomfortable with the growing pointedness of this situation here and now.

The father charged up to the counter and loudly demanded that his daughter receive her boarding pass ahead of these 'other' people.

It happened that many of the people waiting in line had missed a connecting flight due to the lateness of the incoming one and were having to be rescheduled for flights with as many as five changes. All these flights were international, and most required transfers. Well, if one flight is missed, the several subsequent connections must domino.

One proper and duly tired Englishman said to the father, "And don't you think we'd like the same? What is it you think we're all waiting here for?"

The father heard nothing but his own voice. I was amazed at his power of concentration and strength of purpose. The implied and expressed anger of dozens of people in line bore no effect that I could see, and somehow his electricity charged the counter manager enough that the daughter received her boarding pass although no one else received one.

My wheels have apparently never squeaked.

Lenny and Evvy were like cartoon characters. He was no more than five-two, she an inch taller. They, too, were in their seventies. I was aware that I had come from New York and it was December, and he had come from Miami, but it did look mighty strange to see this man in bright red running shorts. Lenny's legs were so extremely bowed, one would have thought he would go to great lengths to avoid shorts; in addition to the shape of his legs, the wrinkled skin on his thighs flapped. Most people who walked by did double-takes of the kind in vaudeville.

Evvy kept walking outside the terminal because she needed to smoke often. Lenny constantly made jokes of the vaudeville-circuit variety. He was like a *tummler* from the overlooked Borscht Belt third-rate hotel variety. A *tummler* was an emcee/comic/social director of the bygone Jewish Catskill milieu, known for telling double-entendre jokes which were always off-color and in questionable taste. While some fine comedians traveled that route on the way to success, the third-rate ones were generally offensive. Here lay Lenny, telling jokes so old and obvious that someone else always threw in the punchline before him in the hopes he would get the message that his material was archaic. Nothing stopped him.

Two and a half weeks lay ahead.

"Are you Bob, our guide?" asked one quiet woman.

"I am."

"The papers we received said you would take care of our problems."

"I will if I can," I smiled.

"I've lost all my tickets," she said simply. "I've looked everywhere."

"Are you sure?" I asked in spite of her last statement.

"There's no place left to look," she said without expression.

"Let me see what I can do." I managed my way to two women behind a counter next to the one that was supposed to serve our check-ins. After explaining what happened, they said they would re-issue the tickets, of which there were eight, at a cost of fifty dollars. When I explained that, in turn, to the woman who had lost the tickets, without a hesitation or expression she came to the counter, and the re-issuance was negotiated. Simple as that. Actually, that wasn't much of a charge, when you think about it.

Everyone was getting tired of looking at the flight schedule monitor to see if our flight would ever be posted. We finally learned that the midnight flight would depart at four A.M. I steeled myself against Bela's possible comment.

For many, such as myself, a half-day had already been spent in getting to Los Angeles and waiting this long. With seven-or-so waiting hours ahead of us, people were not at their best.

Manny and Flo were among the last to join us. Luckily for me, they voiced no complaint about the wait. That would have been grossly unfair, since the very-punctual had been waiting so long. Instead, I was soon to learn that Manny would spend this trip letting me know about every cruise and tour they ever took AND how he had worked out the details himself. His sister was in the business, and he had many friends in the business, and he had considered going into it himself because he has had so much experience in it. By now, my mind was getting trigger-happy with the fast-repeating thought that I didn't really want to do this trip anyway. Would I be punished with every negative stereotype that travelers have ever met? What is it about certain self-satisfied travelers that makes them think every other person will be in awe of their endless stories of their travel experiences? They certainly don't listen when the same boredom is poured on *them*. Often, when asked why I retired from tour-leading, though I have a dozen appropriate answers, I reply that I just can't listen to these travel stories any more. I have a difficult enough time when friends tell me about their trips. Just once, I wish someone would say, "I guess you've heard every story." *Why else would I be writing this?*

There are times you feel time just will not pass. You focus on your zero-hour and subtract over and over. As my beard grew on my earlier-clean-shaven face, boarding time did finally happen. Believe it or not, by this time not only had I met each of the forty travelers, I had memorized all names. I told you I am good at that. From teaching, probably. With five classes a day, at the end of each period on the first day of classes, I was able to call each student by name. So here I was, standing at the entrance to the jet-way, acknowledging each member of my group upon entrance. The flight to Fiji would take ten-and-a-half hours. Would it be without incident? Please. Surely everyone would sleep.

The flight, as every single flight of the entire trip, and there were eight, not counting getting to and home from LAX, was perfect. No one could fault anything about Air Pacific, which took us to and from Down Under, or Qantas, which got us from city to city while there. The granddaughter's father had said the airline sucked. Nothing could have been farther from the truth. Waits in airports and flights themselves seemed endless, but the quality and service were without flaw.

Bette was from England originally, but she had been living in the States for most of her seventy-plus years. Her over-biting mouth was almost always in a smiling state and wet at the corners. Her constant over-sweetness was like eating a jar of raspberry syrup, and it was obvious that she did everything possible not to lose her English accent. She was certain that she wowed everyone she met with cuteness. One ten-minute visit was enough for the trip.

"Someone will have to carry my bags," she announced with a smile. "I've had an operation on my shoulder and cannot lift them."

I wished she had stated that differently, in a way that made it other than a given. She had not asked for help, she had not expressed awkwardness; she presented a fact: someone would have to carry them. Me? No. With the details I must attend to at each airport arrival and departure, it was enough that I had my own lugage. Who then? Whom did she have in mind?

Earlier in my travel career I would have taken care of her bags, myself, because I was that stupid and agreeable. Even now I would have gone to some effort to help her. But her pronouncement, her taking it for granted, struck a nerve. Through the end of the trip I never learned how her luggage got transported. I had given her the okay that both her check-in and carry-on would be handled by all hotel and airport porters, however, and so they were, in spite of the fact that only one check-in was to be accounted for, and the carry-on was to be handled by the passengers at all times.

Bette took none of the optional trips, so I did not see her as much as I saw most of the others. She spent most of her time, though, with Anne, a totally friendly, good, cheerful sweetheart of a woman, a union I could not understand except that Anne was totally agreeable to most things anyway and was, I'm sure, the total reason for the success of the friendship.

As it happened, upon arrival at the airport in Fiji, Anne's check-in did not come through. It was the only bag that had not made it all the way. The claims system in the airport was so poor, it took close to an hour before she was able to put in the claim at all. Meanwhile, the other passengers were sitting in the bus, waiting. I could not send the bus ahead without Anne, nor would I leave her there alone. I asked the passengers, who already had impatience due to the chaos in LAX, followed by this ten-and-a-half hour flight, to imagine what they would do if the lost bag had been theirs. If there was any disssension, I never learned of it. Certainly I was aware that they had to think it was another hour lost. I assured them they would not lose the day's tour, but I do know some had counted on the rest-time schedule upon arrival.

Anne took the loss in stride and said she wasn't worried. That's Anne. A number of people offered her clothing in the meantime.

As was my practice throughout the entire trip, I collected the flight coupons for the next flight each time we waited for the current one, so that, once in the air, I had everyone's coupons AND SEAT REQUESTS to hand in at the reservations counter to get processed in advance for the next flight. Though there was time to hand them in in the airport in Fiji, there was no personnel to take care of that. I presented them to our efficient guide, who promised to get it done before our next day's departure.

Dinner was included in the price at our Fiji Hotel, and everyone enjoyed the tropical atmosphere. At the table next to mine, sweet Bette was abrupt with a woman sharing her table. The woman, who later turned out to be rather outspoken, herself, was so taken aback (as, frankly, was I) she was speechless. Bette stated that she, herself, had the floor, so to speak, and the woman would "get over it." I don't even remember what was said; it was small, but it *was* insulting. What I learned from it was how thin-skinned Bette was not.

I checked that the flight coupons were processed, and they were. Though the passengers got the seats they had requested–by some miracle–some asked for changes for the next flight. At this point, I had to announce that it was miraculous enough to get their requests fulfilled, but to expect forty successes on each flight was doubtful enough; if they were then going to change their requests, it would be mad.

Estelle insisted that the three of them, herself, her husband and their granddaughter, be seated together. The request was totally understandable. I would have preferred it if she had asked me rather than demand it as divine right. She had also told me that having to pay a departure tax meant that for them it would be times-three. Well, there were three of them; did she expect cheaper-by-the-dozen? Earlier, she told me that the travel company did not give her a discount for the third person in the room, and she did not think that was fair. Frankly, neither did I. Then she said, "There had better be three beds in the room, not two beds and a cot, or you're gonna hear from me!"

I swallowed the words "Fuck off" at that point. Her expectations were logical, but I was beginning to hate this woman for her manner of speaking to me. She took this tour strictly because it was the biggest price-bargain she could find. There was no other reason. But she planned ahead of time to hate everything, and she was turning her hate to something I felt the need to ricochet. I had never encountered anyone like her. Having been told over and over through the years that I had the patience of Job and was so kind and understanding and accepting and that I let people get away with murder, I was beginning to feel the urge to commit it.

Too many times it happened that when I would announce the time of departure, she would say, "But I thought you said . . . " or "but you said earlier . . . " It reached the point where I would say to the group, "Did anyone hear me say that?", and even though the agreement with me was unanimous, she would frown, as if to say they're all lying.

From Fiji we flew to Brisbane where we connected for Cairns. Once more I was not able to hand in the flight coupons for our next flight, so I just kept them with me. It was important to get this group's boarding passes ahead of time; there were too many to start the processing upon arrival in the airport. So when I could not submit them at the airport, the first thing I attended to upon the group's getting their room keys and all, each time we entered another hotel, was the faxing of the passenger list to the proper airport personnel. It was not always easy. Because the faxing could only be done from the reception area, I had to do the calling first, to make sure someone was available to receive the fax. Then I would have a hotel person fax it, and I requested, each time, that the airport people call me back to assure me they had received it. My own belt-and-suspenders proof of accuracy. The phone-fax-phone system was not always available; the timing was not always suitable. It was not something I could do from my room because there was no fax there. Occasionally, I would have to phone from my room, get the okay for the faxing, then charge down to reception to get to the fax, hoping it was available, then charge back up to my room to get the confirming call. The people at the airport could not be expected to account for a slow or unavailable elevator. A simple process is not necessarily simple. The processing, though, of those boarding passes, was crucial. Forty people and fifty bags in the airport, eight times over, is not a snap, and there was not a small handful of the group sensitive to the process, the work or anything else. Each person wanted immediate, first-class service. How I appreciated the occasional ones who knew I was doing my best, and what a thankless job it was. It was the only time I really felt wasted. You don't need plaudits for a trying job done, but you also don't want to feel totally taken for granted. Could these people imagine at all what it would be like were I not to take care of these taken-for-granted details? I am not in the habit of feeling like a martyr, but I did kick myself for having taken on this particular trip. The camel's back.

The following morning, two women from the local tour company were in the lobby to sign up everyone for all the optional trips in Australia, regardless of what city they originated from. It took a couple of hours. Most people signed up for most trips. Three couples signed up for nothing. Estelle asked me if her granddaughter would get the trips for half-price, because she saw in a travel guide that children were half-price. I assured her that if the guide said that, then so it would be, and it was.

We would be in Cairns for three nights, a welcome thought in view of the hectic travel schedule up to this point. For most people it had meant a flight to Los Angeles, and then there was the grueling wait in the airport, the long flight to Fiji, then flights to Brisbane and Cairns, and now, finally, a chance to unpack.

Two Jewish women traveling together, without their husbands, took a liking to me. And they were enjoyable—mostly. They had been friends since childhood, lived on opposite coasts in the States, and got together to travel.

Elly was hefty, lively and vocal: Margolit was quite lovely looking, quiet and forgetful. Elly was punctual and ready to go at all times, ebullient. Margolit had to be prodded to be on time and required being told everything took place fifteen minutes earlier than it did. Even at that, when she arrived at the bus, she would generally remember that she had to check something back in the hotel. On the first evening out, she lost her passport. No hysterics followed, and she proceeded to enjoy the full day of touring that followed. Anne, whose luggage had still not been found, remarked that people kept telling her how calm she was, in view of her luggage not having turned up. Her answer was, "It's only *things.*" When she learned of Margolit's losing her passport, however, she remarked that that would have made her panic. Ironically, she had been in the same shop the previous evening when Margolit had lost her passport, and she had remembered a saleswoman mentioning finding a passport. She went back to the store and was able to retrieve the passport, Margolit having given her a signed letter requesting same, occupied with something else to prevent her going herself.

Additionally, Margolit had left her camera in the airport, and when she returned for it, it was still there. Once more she had not been concerned. I told her I really enjoyed her company but we could never be friends. I would go nuts with that casual forgetfulness. Some time later, when the bus had let us off at the large Victoria Market (a square block of dozens of stalls beneath one roof) in Melbourne, she stated, "Oh, I could never handle this. I would get lost in there."

"Well," I replied, "you have three choices: Stay with someone who's not afraid of getting lost; walk in one straight line to the end and then just turn around and come back; or don't go in at all."

At the allotted time, when everyone was on the bus, she was the sole absentee. I went back and somehow found her. Which of us was not upset?

Two other women sharing a room also had to restrain themselves. They had started off seemingly well-suited, but their ways were too different, and it was the differences they seemed to center on. Each complained about the other's room habits. One was too messy, the other too constricting. One resented the other's pill-intake; in turn she was resented for her lack of understanding. These two women had been strangers who were matched for the trip to share a room and, therefore, the expenses. In the beginning it seemed like the perfect matchmaking, but pecking order punched a hole in that.

When you are the leader of a group traveling as this one did—all strangers with only their interest in the country in common—you soon learn that people tell you many things you would not know if you were just one of the passengers.

I had told them the first day that one of the joys of traveling is the people you meet on the trip, hopefully encouraging them to make new acquaintances that would turn into friendships. So many friends of mine are a result of travels together, I hoped it would happen to others. But many people are private and, if they open up, it is, somehow, to me, rather than to each other. As a result, the point is reached wherein I begin to learn more than I choose to know about some people. And, logically, I suppose, what you learn is the part you don't want to learn. When two roommates get along well, they rarely talk about it. But if they are at odds, those odds need to be shared, and the group leader is targeted for that. The job is not glamorous, I repeat, but there is something about it that makes the travelers want to talk especially to you. And more than anyone I know, I accepted that role gracefully and willingly—at least till this luckless trip.

One semi-retired couple from the south greeted each day with a smile. In their sixties, they seemed as lovey-dovey as newly-weds, and it gave me joy to watch them. As the days passed, however, I became aware that they did not mingle. At breakfast, they sat by themselves, and, while touring, were slightly apart from the group, but always in the front. Others, in time, remarked that they did not rotate their seating on the bus, as I had requested when we met. I always ask the passengers to vary their seating each day so that everyone gets an opportunity to sit in every area of the bus. I refuse to regiment it by saying something like, "Each day those on the left move two seats forward and those on the right move two seats back." I assume adults will be adult, and it had always worked.

Now, each day someone would remark that the southern couple clung to their up-front seat. Rather than pin-point them, I made another announcement, as if I were speaking in general, not knowing there were violators. When, after another day or two of no change, I made one more announcement about the democracy of seating, Mrs. South came to me at our first stop and, with her ever-present smile, quietly said, "If someone is complaining about our seat, let them get their asses down here early, as we do, and sit where they want."

I remembered how the mere word "damn", coming from Ethel Barrymore, was more shocking than a loud, long string of four-letter words from anyone else would be. This genteel, gentle southern woman flabbergasted me.

We never left late because I had established the rule that we would wait for no one, but Margolit was consistently the last person on the bus, always with some kind of bag and knapsack. There were always remarks that she was late. Late she was not, last she always was. So it seemed that she was late. But she was never ruffled.

Bela's wife and daughter, Ljuba and Ilona, soon became known as the shoppers, not only of this group, but of any group I had ever had. No matter where we went, they came back to the bus with huge packages, buying every kind of clothing imaginable. They never appeared in the same outfit twice, and every day people waited to see what they would be wearing, always something flamboyant and dramatically feminine, as in the movies of the thirties. They wore huge picture hats not seen since those days, and one had to smile at their pizazz. Their taste was no one else's, but it was right for them. It did seem odd to see these women, dressed to the nines, including stockings and dangling, glittering earrings, as we toured primitive villages in Fiji and the native areas outside Cairns. But the two women enjoyed themselves so and were having such a good time, that I felt the joy of their joy. Even the excessive makeup seemed right after a while, and I couldn't imagine them looking right without it. They created a picture that everyone watched, no matter where we went.

The three of them, Bela included, were intense about seeing their luggage loaded on board each time we left a hotel. In spite of the fact that I checked each person's baggage meticulously, they would not board the bus until they saw each piece in the hold. Bags lined up at the bus was not enough. At the airports, the same thing happened. Between airports within the countries, only one check-in per person was allowed. In a group of this size, we are able to get away with extra pieces included, and the number of bags grew as the trip progressed, because people were buying. For forty people, there were now fifty-five bags.

At one airport, the official at the counter asked me to have the group move to a different part of the airport as the lined-up bags were processed. Everyone complied except Ljuba, who refused to go until her bag visibly went onto the conveyor belt. I asked her to leave and she would not. Earlier, one of their bags had gotten torn, and she said she insisted on seeing the bags until the conveyor belt took them out of sight. I told her that would not assure her the replacement bag would not get torn. "Please follow instructions." She would not.

At the first opportunity, I took her aside and said, "You have more than the allotted number of bags, and you far exceed the weight limit. If I tell you to leave me alone with the official, I am able to get your excess baggage through without penalty, because I can always say, if questioned, 'Well, she's not available now to take care of that,' and they'll just push it through. Why don't you just trust me?"

Ljuba looked at me with different eyes, and I could see that she realized that, in my own way, I was doing people a favor by asking them simple things without elaboration, things such as the request to move away from the action area, or lining up a certin way when going through customs. I told them to keep their identification badges on when going through customs because when you are part of a group that looks like a bunch of mid-westerners (pardon me, mid-westerners), you are not as likely to look like a suspected cocaine-and-diamond smuggler. After that, she always seemed to pay particular attention to the jewels that came from my lips. Even Bela upped my grade to a B-.

After our three-night stay in Cairns, we moved on to Sydney for three nights. The quiet woman who had lost her tickets informed me that in repacking, she found her originals. Lenny and Evvy discovered a Chinese restaurant near the hotel and praised it. On the second night, I wandered in there with a couple of the people from the group. There were Lenny and Evvy–again. Upon our entrance, Lenny called the waiter by name and asked him to take good care of us; we were his special friends. It mattered not that there was almost no one else in the place, and good service was a given. Lenny, in his short red shorts, wanted to impress someone, and here was his golden opportunity: he could impress the waiter that he knew us, and he could impress us that he knew the waiter. He made his traditional corny, off-color jokes. I felt sad.

Sadder was the fact that I was seated near Manny, who had more cruise stories to try to impress us with. For years I had been able to listen to these kinds of tales. Much as it was, I knew I had disguised my pain at hearing all these impression-meaning stories. For the first time, I worried that my impatience would show. This time all the stereotypicality seemed emphasized and underscored and amplified. Was it really more than usual or was it this trip that was making it unendurable? Had it always been like this? Had I just lost the patience others had always said they could never have, in my place?

When we had left the hotel in Cairns, the man behind the desk said this was the worst group he'd ever seen. At the hotel desk in Sydney, a young man and woman expressed disdain after the group had all gone to their rooms and I was left with my calling/faxing-for-seat-assignments on the next flight.

"How do you stand it?" asked the young man. It was presumptuous of him, of course, but my weariness must have made me prey to his thoughts, and I did not pretend not to understand. So many in the group were requesting so many things so quickly and so loudly. Jeanne, the woman whose roommate was the pill-popper, never ceased to shout. It could be after midnight, and she said what she said as if the listener were across the street. Strangers always turned at her volume, but she was never aware. In the halls, when many were sleeping, she spoke as if she were on a ballfield.

One person could be asking the desk clerk a question, and another would shout over him. Estelle never wondered whether anyone was talking; when she had a question, she simply pushed ahead and crowed her question in that unbearably strident whine. She continued to insist that the morning schedule was what she said it was. If I said, "Bags out at seven," she would insist that I said seven-thirty or eight–or six or six-thirty. Each evening I repeated the morning schedule. I might say, "Wake-up at six-thirty, bags out at seven, departure at eight." She would add or subtract a half-hour somewhere and insist that that was what I had said. A number of people had picked up on that, and then would catch my eye, wink or shake their heads and correct her without turning around. On the first day I had told everyone that I would put in a group wake-up call each night for the next day; if they wanted to over-ride that with a different time, they were to tell the desk themselves. I wondered if Estelle put in a call for her own time, as allowed, and then decided that that should be group time as well. More than a couple of women told me they would push her off a cliff before the trip ended.

Certainly everything or everyone was not bleak. There were sprinklings of pleasant people who needed no excessive attention, who needed no audience, who followed simple instructions, arrived on time, varied their bus-seats, and were all-around good company. What was wrong with them! Occasionally they would tell me they could see how hard a job it was to lead a group such as this. I needed and appreciated the votes of confidence, just for the sake of sanity.

Elly and Margolit did not make a hit with most of the people, and sometimes they were a bit much for me, too, but they were so genuinely good to me that I wanted not to see any negatives that others saw. We even went together to a Friday night service at the Great Synagogue in Sydney, a first for me because in the past it was either closed or I was not there on a Friday. Jewish company, itself, was a first.

My loving and beloved friend Jo was on this trip. From the start she knew the downfalls of this group. She continued her habit of telling me somewhere along the way that the tour was great and she was having a great time. She always worried that I worried too much. I know that she and Regina had some kind of pact wherein Jo let Regina know that she'd watch over me, keep me from getting too excited, overdoing, carrying someone's bags. She was a leveler. She kept me sane by being my occasional company for dinner. Instead of wanting to escape, just sharing her company was a salve. Most other evenings I went straight to my room after dinner.

The southern couple who would not surrender their bus seats tried to eat in a section of the dining room opposite where the group was to be. I was happy that the hotel, and not I, insisted they sit in the designated area. The night we went to see the fairy penguins emerge from the sea at Philip Island, the husband sat on the edge of the boardwalk, where we all were standing, with his feet dangling to the sand below. Everyone was asked not to have their feet there because it would prevent the penguins from traversing their natural course. I passed the word to him from about six people away. I could tell, when he got the message from the woman next to him, that he said, "I don't care," and he sat as he was. The woman looked back to me with a shrug. I did not understand why he was belligerent; he had always seemed pleasant to me. Well, I had passed the message; I could not physically move him. A park ranger then came over and told him, and he had to obey. Adults.

The visits to all places were exciting and beautiful, and the Australians were charming, friendly and funny. It seemed there was no such thing as an Australian without a fine sense of humor. The people and all the land were so clean and refreshing and inviting.

Two Long Island couples were traveling together. The husbands were cousins. They were all in the late sixties or early seventies. As is often the case when couples travel together, they mingle little, if at all, with anyone else. They make no effort to pull anyone in at mealtimes. They talked about purchasing opals, a particularly known item for sale in Australia. They went on the visit to a major opal company, had the salespeople drag out every opal, but purchased nothing. A few of the quiet, unassuming travelers, on the contrary, did make purchases.

All four of these people had an assumed air and spoke regularly of where they had traveled and what they had bought. In a charming hotel we stayed at in Melbourne, one of the wives, upon seeing where we were to have breakfast in the hotel, objected. She had seen a much more elegant dining room on an upper floor, and the restaurant we faced was more like a coffee shop.

"Why aren't we having breakfast up there? There's no comparison in the dining rooms. This is nothing. I'm paying top dollar for this trip, and I want the other dining room!"

The words, "top dollar", rang in my ear. I hate the expression. Moreover, that this budget trip was costing top dollar was a fantasy. It was a marvelous bargain and well worth much more than the cost. But to say it cost "top dollar" was a joke. I had to swallow my natural retort, of course, and said, instead, "I'll find out why we aren't in the other dining room."

The desk manager explained that that dining room was used only for dinner, and this less desirable one was used only for breakfast. When the woman found out that no one else was being given better treatment than our group, she was content to eat where she had said she wouldn't.

I have been in a number of hotels that use a particular dining room for breakfast only and a different one for dinner. It is a practice. The point is that the undesirable room was undesirable to this woman only if someone else might have had something better. Of itself there was nothing wrong with it.

There are travel companies that offer everything there is to offer, five-star hotels, sumptuous meals and the best of all aspects that make up a tour. These arrangements are costly, and there is little, if anything, to criticize. When someone on a trip that costs a fraction of that demands the same thing, it's difficult to swallow.

New Zealand was itinerized with long bus rides, the thought of which bothered many people. At this time of the trip, having been together for close to two weeks, the many hours on the bus came as a downer. However, as they began to fall under the spell of the absolute beauty such as most had never seen, the country itself won them over. Trips to the warm and inviting Walter Peek working Sheep Farm and the spectacularly dramatic Mt. Cook, with its sheer soaring height, and Milford Sound's fiordic vistas of mountain against water flabbergasted them enough to make them feel the best had really been saved for last.

Even Estelle had mellowed. Her granddaughter had become happier on the trip, due to everyone's kindness to her. Halfway through, the girl told a number of people that she wished her grandmother would only leave her alone. That was everyone's cue to give the girl a bit of extra attention, and honey caught the fly. There had been no complaint about the number of beds in their room, so obviously, Estelle's plan to attack never saw fruition. No need. And the girl showed her new joy by sitting away from her grandparents.

Bela and his family had won over the skeptics, as well. His jolliness became obvious as his enjoyment increased. He raised my grade to a B+.

In the morning of almost the last day of the trip, a number of people had lined up outside the hotel, waiting for the bus to arrive, in order to get good seats. The beauty of the country had probably stirred them to wanting more strongly to sit in the front. When the driver opened the doors, Mrs. South made her attempt to get on early, and Manny physically blocked her. She was a large woman, and did her best to push through, but Manny persisted and won.

"You asshole," she said.

"I'm surprised to hear you say such a thing," he retorted.

"But you *know* what it means, d*on't* you!" she fired back.

By the time her husband attempted to join in her defense, Manny and his wife were seated in the desired seats, a duly won battle having ended. Others on the bus showed their glee. It mattered not that they did not have the desired seat but that the South couple had lost rights.

Lenny, in his red short shorts, said, "They were always hogging the front." But when possible, he and Evvy grabbed one of the front seats, as well. I had made the request on the first day of the trip that those who needed to smoke–since smoking was not permitted on board–please not smoke near the bus door, even though smoking outside, because the smoke and its smell enter the bus easily. Evvy always smoked too near the door and had to be reminded. She smelled strongly from the smoke; just passing her in the front on the way to seats in the back was offensive. Since my seat is permanently the one behind the driver, I was constantly aware of her odor.

Jeanne, the vocal woman, could be heard every now and then saying, "Couldn't you smokers stay away from the damn cigarettes for a while? The whole damn bus stinks!"

About two-thirds of the way through the trip, I had taken the mike on the bus and put in a plea to the group to try to get along. I had never had to do that on any other trip. Hearing my own words was strange to me. I asked them to make the best of everything and try to see the brighter side. I know I ended with, "Love thy neighbor," of all things. Although they applauded my attempt, it remained a group of people who did not mix well. Though some friendships did occur, they were few in number.

I thought constantly of home. Each night I subtracted time from the remaining days. Finally we flew from Christchurch to Fiji, where we were in for a four-hour layover. I saw to it that I was the first to exit the plane, and I hightailed it to the desk to get our boarding passes processed for the next flight. Here the group was fully aware of the expediency, because there was a huge line behind me, and I was able to get our boarding passes before anything else took place.

After the long wait, we boarded the plane for our almost-ten-hour flight to L.A. Once on board I felt the pressure leave me. The weight of responsibility left me feeling almost giddy. All I had to do now was to think of home. I would never see these people again.

On trips of my own, I am not tipped. I make it clear to my passengers that they are never to tip me. I know that from time to time some of them wonder, but I explain it thoroughly: it would be something like tipping your teacher or your doctor. However, on trips where I am strictly the guide, the escort, for a group of strangers, the company that runs the trip sends to the passengers a complete packet of instructions which includes a tipping guide, and it clearly suggests how much the escort/guide is to receive. So everyone knows that I am to be tipped. Though my expenses are paid, and there is a commission on optional trips, the tips are my only payment for the trip. Early in the trip I play a private game in which I guess who will be sports and who will be cheapskates. I'm pretty good at it. I guessed correctly that two out of the three couples who did not take optional trips would be cheap. Well, all three stiffed me. I guessed that Bela would turn out to be a sport, and he was. Most people tipped me properly. The cheapskates were Bette and Estelle. No surprise; I had pegged them. What they gave me was miserly. Estelle's tip for three was no more than what I received from one woman, elderly and on two canes, who gave me almost twice the average tip. She had been such a wonderful passenger, I had almost wanted to tip *her.* Our eyes were wet when we parted. The only other person who had stiffed me was the roommate of the woman who had lost her tickets. Oddly, she was the one person on the trip who had asked me (more than once) about getting into the business because she felt she would be good at leading. I hope she leads a group of forty like herself.

Though the three couples who took no optionals were in my care less than the others, I had really worked on this trip, especially in the airports, and it was so tempting to approach them all and say, "Was I really worth nothing?" For one of those couples, I had regularly checked with the airlines for their frequent flyer miles, as they had asked me to. That is not a part of my job. Well, you can't pick your relatives, either.

There was a four-day optional extension to that trip, going on to Aukland. I did not accompany the group because only ten of the people had signed up for it, and the company would pay my way only if a minimum of fifteen people went. This was all arranged before leaving the States.

As with a similar previous trip, one of the couples agreed to act as leaders. I had given them a sheet with the necessary contact names and told them that for that portion of the trip, the driver was also the guide, and it would all work out simply and smoothly because the people who ran the trip were skilled at it. And as with the previous trip, the couple who would act as leaders felt confident and capable. How difficult could it be?

I will admit to some small gloating when I learned afterwards from others that, though there were only ten people to count, as opposed to my forty, it proved difficult; though there were bags for only ten, there was difficulty keeping track of them. The boarding passes I had worked so dilligently to get ahead of time were somehow not available. My seemingly simple job that anyone might feel he could do, turned out not to be so simple, after all. The unnoticed glue that held everything together was not there. I imagined what ease there would be in ushering just ten people, including myself, in a place where there was no traffic anyway. Most teachers feel they could be a better principal than the principal. I don't feel the slightest guilt in smiling.

The uneventful flight back to the States arrived on time; I did not see everyone to say goodbye, and that was delicious. My last responsibility was over. I felt a slight sense of guilt in my attitude, but I reminded myself that I had earned this peace. There was an eight-hour wait for my connecting flight back home. I could endure that. I lost myself in my book, a novel that had nothing to do with travel.

Being met by the family at the end of the flight was especially tasty to me. It was over. I had led my last group of strangers. There was just one more trip I wanted to do.

It seems too simple and obvious to put it into words, but when things have seemed less than right, when a situation has been difficult and decisions crucial, when there wasn't certainty about the light at the end of the tunnel, I have gotten through by remembering to

consider the alternative.

As cool as the other side of the pillow.

13

SO WILL I EVER FIND SHANGRI-LA?

Rerun: When I was twelve, the movie theater in my home town reissued the original black-and-white **LOST HORIZON** with Ronald Colman. It did change my life permanently. Favorites from childhood change, and so it was with everything in my life, but not **LOST HORIZON**. It remains my favorite movie. I have the original Pocket Book paperback of it; I have the video, which I have watched several times, and the effect, though not the same since I know the outcome, still hits me. Because of it I have always wanted to go to Tibet. Often I am asked which, of all the places I have not seen, do I most want to see. Immediately and automatically my answer is "TIBET!"

For many years, when Tibet's borders were closed, there could be no thought of it; it was simply out of bounds. When, after some time, it became possible to enter, I tried to arrange a visit as an extension of one of the number of China trips I led. At the time of my visit to Nepal the borders were still closed, so all I could do was to gaze into the distance and construct it in my mind. When the China trips became popular, I tried to include a side trip to Tibet. Companies that put trips together never included Tibet between the beginning and end of the visit to China. The trips went on to Hong Kong. An optional visit to Tibet meant going back from Hong Kong. I could never get enough people to warrant a venture to that isolated place, and I always had to see the group through to Hong Kong, making it almost impossible to get to Tibet. To go on my own back from Hong Kong always seemed over-involved. So my dream never came to be.

When I decided to retire from tour leading, Peru had just begun to become visible. There had been the years of trouble with Tupac Amaru, and security was always a risk. As with other people, the mention of Peru immediately brought to my mind the awesomeness of Machu Picchu. How many hours had I pored over lavish coffee table volumes of the breathtaking Shangri-la of the Andes? I would be doing one final trip. Wouldn't this be the time to do Peru? Go out with a bang? My mailing list was peppered with people who wanted the offbeat experience.

An opportunity afforded itself when I made a contact through a fine company I had worked with previously. They were going to try including Peru in their programs. A young woman, Elena, was brought in from Lima specifically to handle trips to Peru. I thought she would be swamped with requests, but only one group before me had showed any interest, and that group was not even American. I had many phone conversations with Elena to work out details, since this was entirely new territory for me. I had many questions and often had to wait for her to call Lima to get answers. Inasmuch as this would technically be the first American group to go through this company, Elena and the company wanted to be extra sure that everything went well. Having used this particular firm before with outstanding results, and having established a fine rapport with them, they were anxious for it to be a success. I had brought them many satisfied clients.

I went into New York to meet with Elena and quickly learned how eager she was to create a tour that was everything I had wanted. The president of the company told her to give me special treatment, and I felt it from the start.

The traditional plan was worked out wherein we would fly into Lima, leave the next day for Arequipa for a few days, then on to Puno for a few more and, finally, wind up in Cuzco, from which point we would visit Machu Picchu and Ollantaytambo. The routing was an obvious, traditional one, planned to build excitement as the tour progresses.

We worked out all the details of time break-ups, hotels and itineraries. As questions arose, I called Elena because I had had no experience in Peru, and there were no examples I could follow or people I could ask. To be a virgin group can be somewhat unsettling. There were no pitfalls I could anticipate, so

I wanted to be certain I could handle anything that might go wrong. What if a liaison did not appear at the airport to meet us? This trip was offbeat. Elena assured me all would go unruffled. She even gave me her parents' names and address in Lima.

The perfect group signed on. Favorites from all the past years joined this adventure. Jo and Bootsie and her boys and Texas, and Eileen from the India trip, as well as previously unnamed favorites from the first trip to Egypt. If I had set out to assemble the ideal group, I could not have come up with a better one. Even a few new names turned out to be gems. I truly lucked out with the personnel.

Our one-day tour of Lima was perfunctory and fine. Our one-night hotel stay was at the only five-star hotel on the trip. We left for Arequipa via Aeroperu. Here our hotel was as unimpressive as any I have ever stayed at. El Misti, the volcanic mountain that everyone gazes on with awe, was impressive, but my lasting memory of Arequipa is the Monasterio Mysterioso, at which young girls from Spain, during the days of Spanish rule, lived as nuns with servants. It was considered a luxury, and the girls were from families of great wealth. Though their accommodations may have had luxurious carpets, as we were told, they seemed like little more than cells. I thought of the long journey from Spain to the far side of South America, the probably arduous trip on the ship, and the cloistered life in this remote spot and wondered why. The monastery was walled away from the city, and though it contained all necessities for the time, I could only think of it as a punishment, sending a daughter halfway around the world to live in a grotto. The prestige involved haunted me as a life sentence.

We were met in our third Peruvian airport, Puno, by a guide who was different from all we had ever known. His name was Eduardo, and he had the appearance and manner of a country fisherman. He wore a fedora and a too-small sweater whose tan wool color varied every few rows. He proudly told us his wife has knitted it. Inasmuch as all the knitwear we came upon throughout Peru was stunning, this poor sweater was a pitiful sight. His clothing in general was shabby. More important was his wonderful, warm, kindly manner. We learned that his English came from radio news reports. He was conscientious enough to have become much more than proficient just by learning from the radio, and although his speech was sometimes halted, it was excellent. It was also obvious that he was anxious to give us the maximum in guidance. Tour groups were fairly rare, and he was happy to have this opportunity.

We all wondered from time to time what medical facilities were like in this area, where it was easy to see there was not much wealth. We were astonished to learn from Eduardo that there was one doctor for 10,000 people. It was not a shocker to him, of course, and he added that they all take care of each other, and that many medicines and remedies were from natural sources.

We knew ahead of time that Puno was one of the highest places in altitude, almost 13,000 feet, which might cause breathing problems. So far everyone was okay. All instructions said to take it easy the first day and to drink coca tea, a drink made of the leaves of the coca plant. The leaves are chewed on by women in labor in order to ease the pain. That should tell you something.

We arrived at a charming Spanish colonial building which was our hotel. It had only three levels, and there was no elevator. I noticed that each flight of stairs was especially long, the stories high. As Regina and I walked up to our room, one flight up on the second level, we each found we had to stop halfway up in order to catch our breath. It happened each time we ascended the stairs, but other than that there was no noticeable altitude problem in Puno. Dinner that night was served at a banquet table in the long colonial dining room where only one other table was occupied with guests, and where three musicians played Peruvian music for almost the entire meal. I found the food fine.

The next day we left for a sailing on Lake Titicaca, the world's highest navigable lake. On our way from the hotel, Eduardo had the coach stop in the middle of town, where he and I got off and walked a block away to where there was a large group of merchants selling various goods on abandoned railroad tracks, around which all the ground was wet. The tracks themselves served as a platform above the wet ground. We went to a candy merchant. Eduardo suggested I buy candies for the children we would see on the floating islands, the Uros. I bought several pounds of assorted wrapped candies—hard candies, lollipops, gum, all the kinds we used to call penny candy at home. I noticed all the children with their merchant-parents, looking at me buying so much candy. Then Eduardo and I returned to the coach.

As we arrived at the point where we were to board our boat, a launch just the right size for our group of thirty, we noted a spanking-clean structure the size of a child's very small bedroom. Large clear letters designated it as a health station for tourists. I thought of Eduardo's words about the scarcity of doctors for the populace. I also recalled the picture of all those sellers, probably black marketeers, back on the tracks, spending their day waiting in the mud, huddling, wrapped in their brightly colored ponchos. Who were the buyers?

As our boat sailed into the lake, we saw a large open boat, like an cinemascope rowboat, pass us in the opposite direction, filled to the brim with bicycles. People from the floating islands were commuting to the mainland to work. And then we saw the islands themselves. They were literally made from totora reeds, thatched thickly, and though they were fairly stationary, they were, indeed, floating.

We docked alongside a large one. What is large? It was probably a hundred feet across in each direction. On it were huts the inhabitants lived in. Of course there was nothing in the way of electricity or even modernity. The lake was the bathroom and the water supply. There were a few iron pots for cooking. Food was fish and vegetation. I saw nothing in the way of furniture. The thatched roofs slanted for the rain water to escape or be captured for use.

Tourists provided income, so the people provided handicrafts for sale. There were primitive weavings and carvings, none of which was anything I would ever want, but, like most people, I would suppose, I bought several things in order to help the people. I constantly wondered how rarely there might be tourists. We saw so few anywhere else.

There was even a museum on the island. It was perhaps ten feet deep and five feet wide, but it was there. It housed half-a-dozen stuffed birds. The islanders tried to provide something else for the tourists. They live there year-round, and one of the little islands does have a school.

As the underneath reeds of the islands rot away, the top is laid with more, so that each island is replenished by regularly equaling the disappearing bottom with an ever-new top. Legend has it that these Uro Indians had black blood which helped them survive the cold, harsh conditions they lived in. Today the Indians are a combination of many Peruvian descendants. The poverty is depressing, yet the children–always the children–captured one's heart with their cuteness, charm and, yes, happiness. They had so little; I thought of the waste at home.

When Eduardo took us to visit Sillustani, a lonely, forlorn area of burial monuments, he alerted us to the number of guinea pigs scampering aroung the ruins, and we were reminded that guinea pig is a popular food in Peru. A couple of people gasped at the reminder, but east is east . . .

Our hotel was located on a narrow corner. Each time we arrived there, we noticed a half dozen Peruvian women knitting sweaters, dozens of which were always on display. This one night it was raining. The women were huddled in doorways, but they were nevertheless there, waiting for us. My eye caught one particular sweater in color and style I liked. They beckoned for me to take it into the lobby to try it on, and I did. The fine, silky, baby alpaca wool liked me. Regina and I bought a few sweaters. I thought of Eduardo's poorly made, hard wool sweater. I hoped my group would tip him well when we left.

When it was time for us to leave Puno for Cuzco, Eduardo saw us to the railroad station, and I noticed how cautiously he guarded and checked our baggage. From city to city we had gone by air, but I had been advised to see the beautiful countryside via the train from Puno to Cuzco, even though it would be a lengthy trip.

Our goodbyes to Eduardo were almost tearful, and then we were off. The ride turned out to be twelve long, bouncy hours. When food was served, we had to hold on to whatever we drank to keep it from spilling. Two seats faced two seats on this rattling old train, with a table between the two sets of people in those seats. All thirty of us were together, being jiggled and bounced. The lavatory at the end of the car was primitive and filthy, with a door that not only would not lock but would not stay closed. Its floor was soaking wet from urine.

The beauty of the scenery did make the trip understandable, but inasmuch as we would face another train ride from Cuzco to Machu Picchu, I would have preferred to eliminate this one, especially in view of the fact that it took half a day. I want to experience everything there is to experience in every different country, but I did not love this ride. However, this wonderful group took everything in stride, and that helped.

Our final hotel was an exciting construction, with all rooms different—a palace turned into a tourist place. And there was an elevator.

Cuzco was fascinating. Sacsayhuaman (Americanized in pronunciation to "Sexy Woman") was a thrilling place to visit. A fort created of gargantuan stones in zigzag fashion, resembling a puma's mouth if seen from above, it was the site of one famous Incan resistance to Cortez's conquerors. It had protected the valley below. But it rained almost the whole while we were there. It had almost never rained in a long career of tour leading. People always remarked that I seemed to assure good weather. It had rained only once that anyone remembered, on a visit to Athens and to Delphi, but it was short-lived, and that was really all there had been. Now, though, the rain was real. It was not miserable or very cold, just annoying and inconvenient. I had to use that cheap, broken umbrella I had carried for years.

The Temple of the Sun, Koricancha, was thought-provoking. It was important to know the story behind what you looked at in relation to what had been and what they were doing in terms of reconstruction. The Spanish conquest of the Inca took on new meaning when one measured by what was there and the knowledge of what had been confiscated. The story is not unlike others throughout time and the world, but the plight here touched a nerve. Hordes of gold, sheaths and statues, were ripped from their places and melted down by the conquistadores. The place had been stripped and a church built on its site, the original huge-rock foundation walls of the Incas serving as the base for its new home.

And finally, we were planning our trip to Machu Picchu, the raison d'etre. During that first night in Cuzco, I awoke and could not fall back to sleep. I was experiencing difficulty breathing. What could this be? I was all right in Puno, which was much higher. We had descended a couple of thousand feet on our trip to Cuzco. Why would I first now have trouble? The windows were open, and I was aware of the noise outside. I began to clock my breathing bouts. Every minute and a half I had either to inhale deeply or exhale in a long stream. There just seemed not to be enough air. I did not want to wake Regina, but she has always had a sixth sense about me in times of physical difficulty anyway, and I was unable to be absolutely silent with this breathing system I had to work out.

In the morning I was okay. I asked if anyone else had a problem. Just one woman mentioned it, and she was accepting of it. I drank coca tea, but I hated it. I hated its smell. At the desk they had a tank of oxygen for such an emergency. I asked that they reserve it for me for the following night, just in case. They also changed my room to a quieter part of the hotel. I never ask for a room change.

Then we set out for what everyone came for: Machu Picchu. The train ride was four hours long, but a wonderful ride. When you start out, on this narrow-gauge system, the train goes forward for about five minutes, then reverses for five minutes; forward again for five minutes, reverse again for five minutes. I don't know how many of these back-and-forths there were, but what was happening was that the train was zigzagging its way to a higher lever. By the time it took off on its direct route, some twenty to thirty minutes later, we were able to look down to our starting point and realize that we had ascended quite high from the beginning. And then we were on our way.

There were two stops on this trip, at each of which many hawkers appeared with irresistible woolens. I had already bought the sweaters, plus several blankets and scarves, earlier on the trip, so I was able to look beyond. But then I spotted one hawker with the tiniest baby booties I had ever seen. They were made of pure white baby alpaca. My children were grown, and as yet there were no grandchildren, but I had to have those booties.

My group occupied the entire car. The sellers were selling through the window from outside. I hoped no one would get to those booties. Finally they were at my window, and I bought them. And since I now have grandchildren, I smile at the thought.

Soon we were paralleling the Urubamba River, crashing ahead on our left, muddy and turbulent. It looked menacing and threatening. We had just read in the newspaper a few days earlier about a landslide caused by the violent waters, and many deaths as a result of it. Now the picture of it made it eerily understandable. Fodder for many cameras.

At last we arrived at the base of the mountain we were to ascend. We boarded a bus that surely came from one of the movies of the thirties about escapees in danger in some far-off, forgotten, wartorn jungle land. The road up the mountain is total hairpin zigzag and mostly unpaved. To make matters frighteningly worse, every turn was covered with eight inches of mud, and every time the bus made its upward turn there were gasps from everywhere. Would it slide off the edge this time?

It takes just under half an hour to reach the point of disembarkation. It is a long time and way to keep your Adam's Apple inside. And then there is the arrival.

Our guide led us on a narrow path on our way to Shangri-La, first through a toll station where our tickets were collected, then on a path with no barrier to keep one from falling off the face of the earth.

In *Lost Horizon*, the only evidence that Shangri-La is right there is a simple, crude post, raggedly tied to another piece of wood, just as a marker of a spot. Here I was, about to see my Andean Shangri-La, when before me on the right was that wooden arrangement from my movie. I wondered if anyone else had the mesmeric picture I had. It was beyond *deja vu*. I had to stand for a moment. And I had to take a photo, of course.

We continued our foot ascent until we reached that point that gets everyone, the point from which you look down and say, "This is it." It is your first view of that most recognizable scene which represents Machu Picchu to everyone, down in the hollow before Huayna Picchu, the other mountain across the way. The weather had been perfect, affording glorious views no matter which way you looked, but this was February, the rainy season, and the scene changed every time you looked around. Clouds formed and quickly moved. Rain came lightly and left. Blues turned grey and blue again. The colors of the stones changed from warm to cool. Huayna Picchu disappeared in mist as we looked at it.

Up steps, down steps, up paths, down paths. Here is where Hiram Bingham entered when he discovered Machu Picchu in 1911. Here is the hitching Post of the Sun. Here is the Temple to the Sun. We listened to the guide give us living words from the volumes we had studied.

I do not have religious experiences. I do not discuss religion, as religion, if I can help it, because my views are unorthodox and unpopular. I will say that I had the first mystical experience I ever knew, visiting Machu Picchu. I had waited so long for Shangri-La. This second-best place could not be it. Yet, something was happening to me for the first time. One of those intangibles that cannot be described because there is no formula or outline. I need things you can put your fingers on. I could not put my fingers on whatever this was. I had seen the most magnificent sights (and sites) in the world. The Pyramids, the Great Wall, the Taj Mahal, the mountains of Switzerland, the Norwegian fiords. I was stunned by all, but I cannot say something mystical happened. It was not a feeling that stayed. Now I felt it more than once, something mysterious that just seemed to tease me. Was it the wonder that Conway, a.k.a.

Ronald Colman, felt when the realization of Shangri-La hit him?–the thing that says it's true, but can it be?

We returned to the hotel after the treacherous downhill repeat of the bus ride and the train trip which got us back late at night.

The breathing episode of the previous night repeated itself. I tried taking the oxygen, but I noticed no difference and, instead, waited out the night with all kinds of growing worries: Is it my heart? Can I die from this? How can I worry Regina so? Can I make it? Will I die?

In retrospect everything seems ridiculous. It was not ridiculous. I was really scared. Panic certainly does not help that kind of situation, but how do I avoid panic when it's exactly what I feel? Will the morning ever arrive? And what makes me feel I'll be all right even then?

Morning did arrive, and for whatever reason, the two-night problem did not present itself in the daylight. I knew I wasn't crazy, but what was the explanation? The woman who had said she had felt the problem told me she was all right now, as well. But she had been drinking the coca tea; I had not. Whatever it was, all was fine on our last visiting day. We were going to Ollantaytambo. The necessary climbing of this Incan fortress/city was more challenging than Machu Picchu. For this visit, Regina did not join me. She felt the breathing problem would be too tough. Jo stayed with her, as well. It was dramatic to trek up and along this indestructible fortress. My imagination and readings crowded my mind with thoughts of the search for Vilcabamba, and the City of Gold and Incan treasures and the tragedy of such a short-lived society, a doomed people.

Although our trip to Peru was not long, I was not sorry that it was coming to an end. I did not want to think of struggling with breathing; I did not enjoy the lack of hot water in the bathrooms or the wait for what warmth there was, wasting water all the while by letting it run–or trickle, actually, because water pressure seemed to be a problem everywhere except in Lima. Moreover, this was my last trip, and, knowing that, my concentration was beginning to focus on what lay ahead.

The people had all been sweet and charming; the sites were intriguing; the hotels, well, three out of four ain't bad. And now we were flying from Cuzco back to Lima for our connecting flight to Miami and then JFK.

Our liaison in Lima, a happy man who was terrific when we arrived there from Miami on the first day, met us with a smile. He was to take our flight coupons and get our boarding passes. The system was a mess. It was taking forever, and the plane was ready for takeoff before half the group got their boarding passes. I asked him if something couldn't be done to hasten things. Would we all get on? Here comes the sweat.

With the passengers, themselves, getting worried, at the last minute he handed me a bunch of boarding passes, and we scurried to get aboard.

Some time after being settled in the plane, I began to go through all the documents I had, when the realization presented itself to me that I now had no boarding passes from Miami to JFK. We were going to arrive at Miami Airport all right, but what was I going to present in order to get thirty people on the flight from Miami to JFK? In the mad rush to make our connecting flight from Lima to Miami, and the mixed-up system there that took so long, and my request to get us through before the plane takes off, our liaison did not get either our coupons or boarding passes for the last leg of the flight.

I beckoned the airline attendant and presented the problem. She told me she would check on it and get back to me. Time went on, and she never acknowledged it. I asked her a second time, and she said she would see what she could do—as if this was the first time I had spoken to her. Again, the next time she came by she said nothing. After considerable time again, I asked her, and she showed annoyance.

"Are you doing anything about it?" I asked. I can't arrive with thirty people and find ourselves stranded in Miami! In addition, Miami is port-of-entry, and we'll have to go through customs there. How do we handle that without tickets?!"

"I told the captain," she answered briskly, and moved on.

I left my seat and went to find another attendant. The one I found had apparently been apprised by the first one, and spoke as impatiently as the first one had.

"I'd like not to make a scene," I said. "Would you please let me speak to someone in authority? I have thirty people without boarding passes. I'm trying to get this fixed before they find out. They think I have their passes, because I always do. If you don't get this straightened out for me, I'll tell the passengers, and then you'll have *thirty* people trying to do what I'm trying to do!"

Sheez, how I hate to be a squeaky wheel. But sheez, how necessary it has to be sometimes.

A woman in authority then appeared. I re-explained the problem. She disappeared. In five minutes she returned to tell me she had contacted the ground crew; we would be met and helped through customs and transfer.

I had to say, "You're not just saying that to pacify me, are you?"

"I could never do such a thing," she answered. "You would know immediately."

Because I am the way I am—Worry Wart, Nervous Nellie, whatever—I was unable to relax for the whole trip. I could not read, watch the movie, sleep—nothing.

But if things work out, all is forgiven. A pretty and sweet girl who had seen us off from Miami to Lima, and who had remembered me, was there to meet us. Our mess-up was more than made up for because we had help through baggage claims and customs and getting our next flight. The airlines had bent over backwards to make up for the difficulty which was caused by the airport in the first place, back in Lima. All was well with the world again.

Airports.

And now that it's over . . .

14

WHAT WILL I MISS?

Certainly I will miss traveling all over the world with all my expenses paid, which is how I came to lead groups in the first place. I could never have done so much traveling–all to places I chose myself–if I had had to pay for it out of pocket. There were a couple of times that the free trip was the total gain; most times, however, profit was excellent. Mostly, the greatest benefit of "my job" was getting to see the world with, for the most part, people I enjoyed traveling with and who will always be a part of my life.

.... The impression I always get when I stand in the Grand' Place in Brussels or at the wharf in Bergen, Norway or in the square in Prague. It's mesmerizing when I see history books and beloved novels stir on the back shelves of my mind and recall the backgrounds of the stories that entranced me when I made my regular pilgrimages to the Ossining Public Library throughout my youth. Especially on rainy days. I had carefully selected romantic adventures from the book shelves and sat contentedly in the oak window seats, devouring as much as I could before taking out the books I thought I could read in the two weeks' allotted time. Everything came to life every time I visited the Grand' Place or its sister squares throughout the most typical of my European travels. Everything modern was almost invisible to me, but my youth returned as I gazed upon the Europe of old in my imagination. On one particular stay in Brussels, my hotel, an old European-style building with old world charm, the *Astoria*, was situated only a few blocks from the Grand' Place. During even brief intervals of leisure time between or after meals, I would walk to the square to see it under every condition of light. Displays of heraldry and old-fashioned costume movies flashed before me, and I almost swayed as I gazed up and around. Surely I must have looked like the typical hayseedy tourist in awe. I could not sate myself. Probably the foremost longing is that sight, that feeling. I did not attach myself more to Belgium or to Brussels in particular than any other place, but the post card picture that represents nostalgia for a time and place seems to be that.

. . . . All the squares in all the towns all through Europe, where I am transported back to the past few centuries in a place that looks nothing like anything we have at home.

. . . . As a country on the whole, Italy. I've been back to Italy more than any other place, and somehow it doesn't matter where I find myself, there I want to stay. The obvious tourist cities thrill me as they thrill everyone else. Who doesn't fall in love with Rome and Florence and Venice? Rome holds spectacular collections of art from the museums and galleries to the Vatican. Florence makes everyone wax romantic with dreams of artists and writers, and one wants to walk along the Arno and take side streets past homes of famous artists and literati. Venice's canals immediately bring the sounds of mandolins and violins and accordians to the mind's ear, and an entire day seems like a dreamland that will fade when you awaken. However, when one goes beyond those places, and beyond Pisa and Pompeii and other relative journeys inspired by friends' and agents' package arrangements, the "other Italy" seems to extend a more powerful beckoning to come hither and to remain. The hill towns, southern Italy and Sicily have been almost painful to leave. When I see abandoned villas in the hills on a coastal drive, the same taunting recurs, saying, "Who says it's too late to move here for part of the year at least?" My fantasies overwhelm me even to the point of erasing the conversations taking place on the bus as vistas blur by. I wander through Taormina in Sicily and say, "Why not spend part of every year here?" And then I say, "Why here? There are a thousand other Italian towns." But does the sea look like that elsewhere? Where is the spot where I can have it all? If I had come here half a lifetime ago and seen this much, would I be living where I do now?

. . . . The marketplaces that lure me to want to buy almost everything I see, whether in the Cloth Hall in Crakow or the souk in Cairo. There is so much I have to have. I have to have it in my house, to be able to look at it and touch it at any time, and recall the place it came from. There is so much I want. How much can I really take back home?

.... The lobbies in all the hotels that look like converted palaces, not the cookie-cutter room arrangement of our modern-day American hotels. So often I think we should not be dressed as we are in the present century. The atmosphere requires the elegance of clothing from times past. Women should sweep past in ball gowns, men in tails.

.... A hotel in Taormina, Sicily, which overhangs the sea.

.... A hotel in Venice that makes me think I can't really be there, but since I am, must I leave?

.... A hotel in Bali, where the walls of the public area are open to the elements, and where the leisure areas with its glorious pool makes one want not to return to the real world.

.... The architecture of all the irregular, crowded streets which cause me to look up instead of ahead as I do at home. The weathered tradesmen's signs outside the shops. Are they any different from a hundred years ago?

.... The cobblestoned narrow streets that exude charm because I don't have to drive there. The clop-clop of horses' hooves as they haul carriages and carts.

.... The ability to think 17th, 18th and 19th centuries because of being surrounded by them.

.... Towns and villas built into the sides of mountains because no one worried about the impracticality of it. No one imagined the look from the air or even the sea. They just are. Driving home with bags of groceries or having furniture delivered were problems that had to be worked out later. Tiled roofs. Steep, winding paths and irregular steps were forms following functions irrespective of the very old people who would be using them. Somehow they were right for what they were.

.... The romance I feel when I just look up from down and down from up, where the Mediterranean fills the space between.

.... The embroidery in the shop windows in Budapest and Szentendre, in Hungary. My mother, born in Budapest, always had one embroidered peasant blouse in her wardrobe. Seeing these beautiful blouses in so many shops recalled her to me vividly. I imagined her as a young girl living in the area. Gone for almost a third of my life, her face emerged distinctly, and I imagine her joy at knowing I was here.

.... The Pragues and Stockholms and Amsterdams and St. Petersburgs and Budapests and dozens of other cities that have canals running through, with enchanting pedestrian bridges crossing them.

.... All the arenas and colosseums and amphitheaters, whether in Rome or Ephesus or Delphi or Taormina. Standing in each of them over and over, there was always the majesty of government and spectacle and public spaces and civic life in thought–how societies so long ago could create such a monumental concept. Hollywood biblical epics gave all the scope but not the "feel". One needs to walk and sit on those stones and to wander through the passageways that lead to viewing areas. The mind will do the rest, removing the weeds and polishing the rough edges.

.... The intimate, offbeat restaurants in offbeat locations that owed their economic survival to tour group visits because they weren't commercial enough for the casual or indifferent tourist. The managing family of so many, where it really mattered that you savored the food that was lovingly, not merely commercially, prepared.

.... The water's edge food from the stands in Bergen in Norway and in Delft in the Netherlands, the food throughout Turkey, and all the food in all the places in Italy. Ah, the fettucini . . .

.... The coach drivers who won everyone's hearts as they maneuvered their monstrous vehicles through streets never intended for such fuel-puffing Gargantuas. Their struggle to speak in a language they did not know, to answer the myriad of questions put to them by so many passengers.

.... My good friend and incredible tour leader in Italy, Gianfranco, whose voice and manner I would steal if I could. Upon arrival for every trip, seeing his welcoming smile as we exited the airport assured me of the perfect tour. It was gratifying to know that every single passenger would have the same appreciation of him, and when returnees accompanied me on the trips, they and he looked forward to seeing each other. I will not allow myself to think that we may never meet again.

.... The music halls that still present nineteenth century programs (I'm hung up on the nineteenth century). I am one who thinks the *Folies Bergere* should never be allowed to close, regardless of what other kind of show becomes popular. There should always be the *Folies Bergere*. Vive la . . .

. . . . Maid service.

. . . . Not having to squeegee the shower after use, as I do at home.

. . . . Not having to clean up after meals.

. . . . Not having to make the bed.

. . . . Old world manners in hotels and many public places.

. . . . London two-decker red buses, brightly painted red phone booths and the Underground.

. . . . The forgotten towns along the Volga.

. . . . The museums that maintain the atmosphere of the times in which they were built, and the collections therein. Such as the Rijksmuseum in Amsterdam and the Kunsthistorisches in Vienna.

. . . . Walking among statuary I studied in college and never really thought I'd see, standing before paintings I'd only seen in slides and prints.

. . . . Staring straight up at the ceiling of the Sistine Chapel, the first artwork I remember from childhood, remembering it with awe before restoration, gasping in disbelief after. I remember the cracks in the plaster from photos I had seen as a child. On my first visit the cracks were an important memory link. On every successive visit, including those after the restoration, the cracks remained important, as if to tell me, yes, it's still the same place.

. . . . Counting the hairpin turns on the Furka-Grimsel Pass in Switzerland.

. . . . Wondering in Norway if there was such a thing as a person who wasn't beautiful.

. . . . Wondering in Sweden if there was such a thing as a person who wasn't beautiful.

. . . . That unexplainable, all-encompassing feeling of belonging when I am on a typically European street (whatever that means), feeling the sensation that makes me understand the U.S.A. Expatriates, dubbed the Lost Generation, the Fitzgeralds and the Hemingways and their crowd, whose books were my attraction to the places to begin with. There is a draw to European culture, just as there was always a draw to European accents.

. . . . All the good things that were definably foreign, the reason for travel to begin with. I wanted what I did not find at home.

. . . . Israel. A part of me remains there. Here in the States, I had bought a sweatshirt once with the imprint "You never really leave a place you love; some of it you take with you, leaving some of yourself behind." I feel that way most about Israel, which I have visited on many trips and where I lived for a year while teaching on a Fullbright Fellowship. On recent trips, all of which were Holy Land trips, and all of which wound up with a four-day stay in Jerusalem, I found myself each evening, walking from my hotel to the busy "downtown" section, where people always gathered in the street. I felt so much a part of it, some latent emotions from my Jewish heritage being touched by some indefinable chord.

. . . . St. Petersburg, which always made me a little sad because I concentrated on the grandeur that used to be, which somehow came to me as I gazed at the boulevards. My father had been born in Pinsk, which I never got to visit, but in St. Petersburg he seemed to be with me. He's been gone for half my life, and, as my mother's face was clear in Budapest, so my father's was in St. Petersburg. Why there, in particular, I don't know. Tricks of the mind. I had promised myself way back that one day I would visit Russia and Hungary "for my parents", who never went back. But because I wanted it so, they were with me somehow, whenever I visited. Each was a teenager when they left. More than a generation later, what likeness could there be? But if you will it . . .

. . . . Some of the most wonderful people in the world, who will always stay in my life.

... and ...

15

WHAT WON'T I MISS?

The responsibility of it all. Unlike tour leaders who may be far wiser than I, I never ever learned not to take everything to heart. (There's got to be some major insecurity glitch in me). I need for everyone to have a wonderful experience. Who could possibly succeed 100% of the time with that attitude?

.... The work. To create a trip encompassing everything imaginable (according to one's own picture of what should be achieved, of course) is far from simple. Include all the sites, flights, transfers, hotels, guides, drivers, meet the time requirements, make sure the institution is open on the day you plan to be there, fill everyone's day with wonder, double-check everything, work it out, come up with the brochure, do the mailings, follow-ups, answer the endless calls, mail, mail, mail, answer, answer, answer. Meet everyone at the airport and be everything to everyone. I loved it, but I won't miss it.

.... The glitches. The worry that the foreign company representative won't be at the airport. It never happened, but the worry was always there. A bus breakdown. It happened only once, but one worries nevertheless.

.... The sometimes necessary, unavoidable long bus ride. The only way to get from A to B, but the ride can be long. Though one can justify that there's no other way to do the trip, there's always one person who complains about the length of the ride. They say afterwards that the visit was an absolute necessity, but the ride is too long. How else does one get there?

.... The incessant talker. The Judy, who must impress. The Lanny, who must tell you how well traveled he is and how he arranges his trips. The Louise, who must tell you what to add on the way because it's only a few miles out of the way.

 .... The person who is late for the bus more than once.

 .... The person who shops too long.

 .... The smoker who smokes too close to the entrance to the bus.

 .... The one who tells you about the last time he was here ...

 .... The one who tells you he got a better exchange rate (is it ever more than a few cents?).

 .... The ones to whom food matters more than landscapes.

 .... The ones who will miss a visit to a once-in-a-lifetime historic site to get their hair done.

 .... The ones who have money for everything but the tip.

 .... Speaking of tips, I won't miss escorting groups for other companies, where my payment, so to speak, is in the form of tips. It's repelling to me to be evaluated in the form of tips. I realize that people work for tips all the time. Restaurant servers are tipped. But it's different on a trip, where you lead the people from home, have dinner with them, spend time with them. You are not merely the guide or tour leader who is met in a foreign country. Plus, there is the plain, ornery cheapskate. He'll pay for anything up front. And he'll pay to eat. But beyond that, even when the information packet clearly lists tips under "other expenses", there's a resistance. I have always found it awkward to accept tips; however, on those trips where I am the escort for a company, tips are the *raison d'etre*. Since the idea is repugnant, that's a big *'I won't miss'*.

 .... The *schnorer* bargainer. The ugly American who just tries to get the price down from a poor seller in a tiny boat next to our cruiser in order to be able to say how well he did. He doesn't even really care about the T-shirt he got for next to nothing. He cares only about the war he won. Does he really think the seller was so stupid that he sold it for less than it was worth to him? And then he brags to strangers on the boat how he "got him down." Everybody wants and deserves a bargain, but only the ignorant would believe that someone "took" the poor "native."

 .... Third World. Very appealing to me and to my following seemed to be the Third World countries. I don't even like the expression, but there it is. I won't miss dirty conditions, stinking, wet lavatories, clinging beggars, foul smells, unsafe water, being stared at, caste systems, decaying buildings, poverty, smoke. I have never been a snob, and my great joy has been my visits to countries where the preceding conditions exist, in which live some of the sweetest people I have ever seen. I have loved the sights, learning about the culture and the differences between us and attraction of the inherent antiquity. But having been so many times to so many places in the so-called Third World, unacceptable as it may sound now, at the end, I won't miss it. I prefer clean. That is certainly not to say that all was dirty, by any means. And much was extraordinary, but I will not miss what I have described.

.... Airports, waiting for baggage claim at the conveyor belts, customs.

.... Spending hours in the airport, waiting to board the plane.

.... Spending hours in the plane, waiting to land.

.... Long trips in tourist class.

.... Hoping to beat the crowd to the lavatory in the plane.

.... Feeling that someone's waiting right outside, and I'm taking too long.

.... Not being able to sleep on a plane because I can only sleep facing down.

.... The person who calls, asks to be on the mailing list, gets all the newsletters which tell of all the trips, then asks for every brochure for every trip, and never takes any trip. She will ask when the next newsletter will be out, in order to be sure she hasn't missed it, then the same procedure begins again. I think there are people who just covet all mailings. Kind of like the person who comes to a free lecture in the library and collects every flyer that's displayed, regardless of subject. These people must love junk mail.

.... The person who calls and asks for me to place her daughter's (or cousin's or niece's) name on my mailing list. It stays there for years and nothing happens..

.... The person who calls for a reservation right after the deadline for signing up. The deadline is clearly specified in the mailing piece, but the call comes late nevertheless.

.... The person who brings an uninvited, unknown guest to the orientation. This guest is not taking the trip, obviously, and yet no explanation is offered.

.... The worry that it might rain. Having had probably a total of four days' rain altogether in all these years, people have come to say, "It doesn't rain on Bob's trips."

.... The "half-couples" (my term for them). The couples whose wives are enthusiastic and whose husbands damn most things. The wives take the pictures, carry the passports, handle the money, make the arrangements, do the packing; the husbands grace them by coming along, carrying nothing while the wife is laden. The wife is gracious and friendly, the husband bored and indifferent. The wife is alert, the husband sleeps.

.... Threats of bad weather on the day of departure. There were times when I could not be sure everyone would make it to the airport. Once on the way, all went fine, but till everyone got checked in . . .

.... The fear of someone getting sick, getting hurt or dying on the trip.

.... Petty arguments among passengers.

.... Suggestions.

.... Schedules.

.... Certain people no one enjoyed.

.... Having to justify.

.... Those Jewish women from the cities, who place too much emphasis on restaurants.

.... Those Christians who, on Holy Land trips, are in constant awe at every Christian site and in every Christian church, but who will not give ten minutes in Yad Vashem, the Jewish Holocaust Memorial in Jerusalem, the only Jewish site visited on a ten-day otherwise-Christian tour.

.... Any of those people, fortunately in the minority, who have closed minds of any type, mainly the bigots.

.... Caring so much that it wore me down.

.... Home. I won't miss home. Any more. I've missed home so much. Now I won't have to, because I'll be there. All the time.

16

AND NOW?

Now I'm going to watch the grass grow, smell the coffee, sit in a rocker and read all those books I've been setting aside. I'm going to remind myself each day that I don't have to be in a certain place at a certain time. I can browse in my favorite hardware stores and book shops. I can fix what needs fixing and paint what needs painting. I don't need to know the current currency exchange or when it's a good time to be where. I don't have to miss any more friends' children's weddings which Regina has had to attend without me. I don't have to ask Regina to tape a particular show on television. I won't keep up with the travel news in the Sunday *Times*. I won't keep checking weather around the world on the Weather Channel. I won't update my collection of travel guides. I will be able to answer "No" without regret when someone asks if I'm still leading trips.

I will have the rest of my life uninterrupted with my sweetie-pie Regina. My kids, Bill and Whitney and John, will be around all the time to brighten my days, and Bradley and Jason, my grandsons, will be spoiled like crazy. They and their parents, Whitney and John, live only a stone's throw away. I'll never tire of baby-sitting while I sing corny songs and, later on, telling them what it was all like.

Sure, we'll travel, Regina and I. But in the U.S. now. Sometimes we'll do our couple-of-nights-at-a-motel thing, where we just search out all points of interest in an historical area; sometimes we'll take longer trips. We promised Bill we'd visit the Grand Canyon with him. We'll go to the movies in the afternoon, have lunch out instead of dinner, go to off-beat places at off-times. We won't care if we get snowed in in the winter or if it rains on our picnic in the summer. There's always another day.

As for retirement in the first place, I opened this book with Dickens' opening line from *A Tale of Two Cities*; I'll close, just as appropriately, with his last line from the book, but with much better prospects than his hero, Sydney Carton (Ronald Colman, again, in the 1935 movie version) had:

"It is a far, far better thing that I do than I have ever done; it is a far, far better rest that I go to than I have ever known."